Scraps, Orts, and Fragments

PIECES OF A LIFE

Michael Rosenthal

ARCADE
PUBLISHING

Books by Michael Rosenthal

Virginia Woolf

Centennial (editor)

The Character Factory: Baden-Powell's Boy Scouts and the Imperatives of Empire

Nicholas Miraculous: The Amazing Career of the Redoubtable Dr. Nicholas Murray Butler

Barney: Grove Press and Barney Rosset, America's Maverick Publisher and His Battle Against Censorship

For all the

ROSENTHALS AND GAULLS

who have contributed so much

to the pleasures of my journey

Copyright © 2025 by Michael Rosenthal

"Garbage, Faculty" first appeared, in slightly different form, in *A Time to Stir: Columbia '68*, edited by Paul Cronin (Columbia University Press, 2018); my correspondence with Ian Buruma appeared in the June 28, 1990, issue of *The New York Review of Books*.

All rights reserved. No part of this book may be reproduced in any manner without the express written consent of the publisher, except in the case of brief excerpts in critical reviews or articles. All inquiries should be addressed to Arcade Publishing, 307 West 36th Street, 11th Floor, New York, NY 10018.

Arcade Publishing books may be purchased in bulk at special discounts for sales promotion, corporate gifts, fund-raising, or educational purposes. Special editions can also be created to specifications. For details, contact the Special Sales Department, Arcade Publishing, 307 West 36th Street, 11th Floor, New York, NY 10018 or arcade@skyhorsepublishing.com.

Arcade Publishing® is a registered trademark of Skyhorse Publishing, Inc.®, a Delaware corporation.

Visit our website at www.arcadepub.com.
Please follow our publisher Tony Lyons on Instagram @tonylyonsisuncertain.

10 9 8 7 6 5 4 3 2 1

Library of Congress Cataloging-in-Publication Data is available on file.

Cover design by Liz Driesbach

Print ISBN: 978-1-64821-146-1
Ebook ISBN: 978-1-64821-151-5

Printed in the United States of America

Contents

Preface	VII
Family Matters	1
Street Games	12
Summer Camp	17
Hubert's	24
Sex in the Fifties for Nice Horace Mann Boys	31
The Choice	38
Janitor	48
"Garbage, Faculty"	54
Academic Assassination	63
Associate Dean	73
The Kovner Bowl	98

My Almost Club Life	104
Should We Meet Today?	115
Step-fathering	118
Board Member	126
My Table at Rao's	134
Seasonal Effervescence	144
Mr. P and Me	150
Hospital Madness	172
A Bad Scout?	178
Death and Friendship	181

Preface

As the audience struggles to comprehend the significance of Miss La Trobe's historical pageant in Virginia Woolf's last novel, *Between the Acts*, that each is part of the whole, the past an inescapable part of the present, a countertruth is simultaneously expressed: "Scraps, orts and fragments: are we, also, that?"

Miss La Trobe provides no answers, but the question resonates. How does one reckon with the achievement of one's life, with its successes, failures, ironies, and humors, opportunities seized and missed, regrets and satisfactions? The organized narrative of a memoir or autobiography is one possible way, but I think there is something to be said for the "scraps, orts and fragments" approach, which gives the reader the chance to put together an experience of a lived life, free from the artful manipulation of authorial shaping. If we are all somehow playing parts written by other people, as La Trobe's pageant suggests, we are at the same time stumbling through a contingent universe without direction or certainty, not knowing where we are going or how to get there. It is this sense of one unplanned particular journey that I wish to convey.

It is a journey that never took me far afield and will no doubt end where it began, in New York, where I was born in 1937 and have lived, with the exception of four years of college and one of graduate school, the entirety of my adult life. The choice of the city was less a conscious preference than the fact that Columbia University took me in 1960 and never let me go, first as a graduate student in the

PREFACE

English department, then as a teaching fellow, instructor, assistant professor, associate dean of the college, and, finally, a full professor. While New York has always been my official address, it might be more accurate to think of me as a citizen of Columbia.

I make no apologies for the random nature of the episodes included here. My enthusiasm for Hubert's flea circus, our punchball games in front of my father's medical office on Ninety-first Street, my first job as a janitor following college graduation, starting my administrative career amid the shooting of the dean of students in the office next to mine, immersion in a post–heart surgery paranoid-schizophrenic haze, being appointed to the board of directors of a New York Stock Exchange company—none of these are intended to fit into a neat pattern. They simply constitute a very partial record and assessment of how one man has managed his almost nine decades on this earth. Coherence is not one of its goals. The person who was twice rejected from the Century Association is also the person who possesses what is allegedly the most difficult restaurant reservation to obtain in New York: a monthly table at Rao's.

If it seems like a bit of a stretch to retreat to sixteenth-century France to find the best explanation of what I hope to achieve here, I can only say that Montaigne's analysis of the motives behind his *Essays* speaks precisely to the aspirations I harbor for my scraps:

> This, reader, is an honest book. It warns you at the outset that my sole purpose in writing it has been a private and domestic one. I have had no thought of serving you or of my own fame; such a plan would be beyond my powers. I have intended it solely for the pleasure of my relatives and friends so that when they have lost me—which they soon must—they may recover some features of my character and disposition, and thus keep the memory of me more completely and vividly alive.

Family Matters

It would probably be unfair to accuse my father of not liking me, even if that is how I perceived it. A more just assessment would be that he liked me—sort of—but simply could not demonstrate it in any way that mattered. Of course, that came to the same thing. Lacking what might be called nurturing gifts, he had no interest in contributing to any kind of positive self-image on his son's part. I am confident it never occurred to him that such a concern might properly belong to the job of fathering. Mothers existed for that. On the other hand, he was an intuitive master of techniques guaranteed to undermine my sense that I might actually exist.

Saturday lunches were a prime example. We lived in a duplex apartment on Central Park West. My father, a physician, spent most of his professional life as an administrator in New York City's health department, while also maintaining a small dermatological practice in the evenings and on Saturday mornings in the suite of offices on the ground floor of our apartment. When he finished seeing his patients on Saturdays, he would come up the stairs for lunch. If my mother was out, our cook-housekeeper had been instructed to serve the two of us our meal in the dining room. During all the many Saturdays we ate together, my father never once talked to me. Lunchtime with his son was reading time for him, an opportunity to catch up on the week's *Life* or *Saturday Evening Post*, the two magazines my parents subscribed to, or simply that day's *New York Times*. I am not sure I ever remember him even looking at me. He read while he ate, head bowed over plate and magazine; I ate in silence, effectively absent. Not exactly the bonding experience shared family meals allegedly can be. I am quite certain he had no idea that conversation with his son might have been a more engaging option than reading, any more than he might have recognized something objectionable in his method of summoning all of us—my mother, my older sister, and me—to get ready to go out: "Let's go, girls," he would inevitably bellow, exhorting us to be on time. I don't want to be overly dramatic about this, but as part of his skill in making me feel he didn't quite view me as a fully fledged member of the family, it must have had some consequences on my tender psyche. Might it have contributed in some way to my childhood migraines? Who knows. At the very least it is safe to say it did not enhance my self-esteem.

Very little I did ever merited his praise, but he had a keen eye out for my failures. After I earned my MA from the University of Wisconsin in 1959 and returned to New York to continue my graduate work at Columbia, he suggested one day in the fall that perhaps I should have my thyroid tested. He said that people with thyroid problems frequently were not even aware that they were performing at a low level. As I thought I had been doing perfectly well in school, and not too badly in life, I asked him what evidence he had as to my difficulties. Much to my amazement, he did have evidence, which he had been surreptitiously gathering for several years. "How many courses did you take in the spring semester of your senior year at Harvard?" he retorted.

"Three."

"And how many could you have taken?"

"I could have taken four, but because I had taken one previously in summer school, I only had to take three, and I wanted to use my free time to read and enjoy my last semester of college."

A self-satisfied look crossed his face; he had already demonstrated the first part of his case: that I was clearly not playing with a full deck. "And how many courses did you take at Wisconsin?" he pressed on.

"I took three each semester, but I also taught one as a teaching fellow."

"I didn't ask how many you taught, I asked how many you took."

I tried to explain that as a TA I was not permitted to take more than three, but he would have none of it. He had proved his point: unbeknownst to me, I was being undermined by my misbehaving thyroid. While I managed to resist his inclination for my medical examination, I never totally recovered from my father's having actually compiled a list of particulars demonstrating my malfunctioning.

There was nothing much I could do about my non-relationship with him except to honor it in all its distance and coldness. In this way I certainly contributed to it. I called him "Father," never "Dad." We shook hands, never kissed. Once, when I was fourteen or so and the two of us were walking to my aunt Mae's apartment, he asked me why we couldn't be friends, suggesting that in fact he understood that something was wrong. I said because we weren't, and that was that. He never tried to approach me again, so maybe I have to admit that I was more culpable in our shared frigidity than I like to acknowledge. In any case, he was not much fun to be around. My sister dismissed him as simply being boring, and perhaps that was the most accurate judgment. It might have been just as well that no conversation was attempted on our Saturday lunches. What could we have spoken about?

I did achieve one major interpersonal victory over him, though, which gave me enormous delight. He had a horrible habit at the dinner table that annoyed me far more than no doubt it should have. When asking for the vegetables to be passed to him, he would invariably say, "Please bean me" or "Please broccoli me," depending on which dish he was seeking. I hated this, for no particular reason, but could not convince him to refrain. One evening, however, I proffered him a bowl of peas and asked if he would like me to pea on him. My sister and mother, who shared my distaste for his behavior, burst into hysterical laughter; he was not amused in the least, hurling his famous, bone-dissolving glower in my direction, what I called his "face attack," but there was safety in numbers and I felt immensely fulfilled and protected from any retribution. It didn't change things—he continued to want to be asparagussed—but I gloried in my momentary triumph.

Needless to say, we never played together, but I remember thinking quite explicitly—it seems almost infinitely sad in retrospect—that you weren't supposed to play with fathers; that is what uncles were for. When Uncle Paul, my mother's brother, came to visit from Schenectady, we would shoot Nerf baskets in my bedroom, an activity my father never attempted. Uncle Willie, one of my father's three brothers, not only scrimmaged with me in my room; he took me to baseball games and even occasionally football games, supporting my all-consuming interest in sports. I can even recall, one specific summer day, when I was five or six, wrestling poolside with Uncle Hank (not a real uncle, but in those days friends of your parents were called uncle and aunt), relishing the physical contact not otherwise available with my father.

If my father wasn't funny or cozy or supportive in any way, he at least knew a lot—or so it seemed to me. Long before the internet came along to settle all questions, my father served as our homegrown Google authority, able to tell us where things happened, why they happened, and when they happened. I never found him an especially incisive thinker, but he knew immense amounts of stuff. You never had to look things up; you had only to ask him. The fact that he was a physician added to the sense of his omniscience. Doctors were esteemed as the highest form of human evolution in our household, a pathology generated mostly by my mother, a bumpkin from Schenectady who'd married the worldly New York City doctor when she was but eighteen and he twenty-nine. Long after she developed into a sophisticated New Yorker herself, an accomplished party hostess and esteemed writer of cookbooks, she maintained her belief in the moral and intellectual superiority of doctors. I remember with acute embarrassment how she would indicate to a maître d' in a restaurant her unhappiness if he had shown her to an unsatisfactory table: "I'm afraid doctor wouldn't like that." After my father died, in 1980, my mother was pursued by various eligible men, none of whom she expressed interest in. When I asked her what was wrong with one in particular, a perfectly reasonable, attractive businessman, she explained, "Once you have been married to a doctor, it is impossible to settle for anything less."

Despite her worshipping at the medical shrine, I think my mother discovered that she had settled for something less than she had expected. Although he obviously spoke to her at mealtimes, he didn't suddenly become much fun for her, either. Rumor has it (from my sister through my cousin Carol through Aunt Mae, my father's sister) that Mother was on the verge of leaving him in 1954 when he sprang a heart attack, an event that more or less locked her into the marriage. She could hardly, after all, disgrace the family by walking away from her sick husband. Instead, she seemed to gain a new appreciation for him, set about writing a low-cholesterol cookbook to provide him with healthy foods—quite a radical notion at the time—which sold pretty well for a number of years, and she began to develop dimensions of self-confidence as a writer. The next twenty-five years were unquestionably the happiest for her.

My first years back in New York, on the other hand, were quite miserable. I hated Columbia, didn't feel I could ever make it as a professor, hated the city. I came to recognize, after a considerable amount of suffering, that it was my head, not my thyroid, that was plaguing me and that rather than accepting my preordained failure, I should try to do something about it. The answer, the only answer I could come up with, seemed to be psychoanalysis. As most of my friends who were not on the way to becoming professors were on the verge of becoming psychiatrists, it was not difficult to gather recommendations of institutes looking for customers for their analysts in training. I assumed one had to be interestingly neurotic but not hopelessly sick, with some capacity for self-awareness. A perfect description of me, I thought, so I fully expected to be discovered as an appropriate candidate. I was right. The New York Psychoanalytic Society & Institute accepted me, and given my lavish $4,000 salary as a graduate student preceptor in Columbia's English department, the fee of two dollars per session proved to be one that I could afford.

My first meeting with my psychiatrist was disastrous. I had clearly spent a good deal of energy imagining what would take place, and had fashioned a scenario that made sense to me: I would step into the psychiatrist's office, we would sit down and chat pleasantly for five or ten minutes, he would explain to me how things would work and what I might expect, and when I felt properly relaxed and comfortable, he would suggest I go to the couch, and we would begin.

None of that happened. We greeted each other, and without another word spoken he waved me to the couch. I was furious. I wanted it to be friendly and nice, and this was not that. No way to treat me, I felt, but I'll show him. I won't say a word. So I didn't, for at least five minutes, an eternity in a psychoanalytic setting. The silence was excruciating, but I refused to budge. Finally he spoke: "Why don't you tell me about your mother?" Much to my horror, and not in the least attempting to be humorous, I heard myself utter the stupidest thing I could have possibly said: "If you don't know her, I really couldn't describe her." As soon as I delivered myself of this idiocy I recognized this was not a way to proceed, even if it did cost only two dollars, so I finally launched into a description, which I finished six and one-half years later. During this time we dealt with migraines, love relationships good and bad, doctoral dissertation paralysis, an unanticipated puppy given as a gift by a girlfriend who then deserted me a week later, apocalyptic career fantasies, the ravages wrought by growing up in a family, and other associated wounds caused by living.

A skillful analysis, which taught me things about myself that I almost certainly wouldn't have been able to figure out without help; success at Columbia, where I moved from graduate student preceptor to instructor to assistant professor; and, I suspect, just the simple act of growing up conspired to render me, at least in my own eyes, a relatively plausible, functioning human being. Now only one big question remained: Was this plausible human being fated to spend the rest of his life alone?

The evidence didn't seem definitive either way. Relationships came and went, with varying degrees of loss and liberation. I specialized in intense ones of moderate duration. Before the era of dating programs on the internet, I thought of myself as the king of blind dates, following any lead that came to me. Old, young, rich, and poor, I took them all to dinner, hope springing eternal. Sometimes they worked out; mostly they did not. While my father had worried that my shoddy academic performance sprang from my diseased thyroid, Mother worried that my dismal marital showing (I was, after all, past thirty and still single) might stem from what was considered then a sexual pathology. "You're not gay, by any chance," she said on more than one occasion, trying to make light of what was clearly a deadly serious issue for her. "No, Ma, not that I know of," I would reply, trying to reassure her.

Ironically, in her quest to have me properly married off, she actually managed to interfere in a relationship in which I was quite involved. A girl I was seeing regularly got a job at the *Grolier Encyclopedia* company, where Mother worked as a writer. My mother was smitten by Dorothy, assessing her as the perfect mate for me, oblivious to the fact that selecting a wife for her son might not please her son. She began extolling her merits to me on a regular basis, imagining that such praise might help ensure her future in the Rosenthal family. Then, one night, when I had been invited home for dinner, she permitted herself to lose all maternal constraint. As we were having a drink, she announced that she wanted to give me a gift, and presented me with a small, neatly wrapped box. I didn't need to open it to know what it contained. While there must be other instances in the vexed history of mothers and sons in which a desperate mother thought it appropriate to propose to her son's girlfriend when he seemed unwilling to do it himself, I certainly didn't know of any examples. But there it lay, folded in tissue paper, my mother's own diamond engagement ring. "Is this a ring for a man?" I said innocently. "No," she replied. "Well actually, thanks, but I don't think I need it," I said, pushing it back toward her. We never discussed it again, and she had to live with the disappointment that the woman she had chosen for me and even in some technical sense proposed to did not become my wife.

Several years later, without any help from my mother, I did decide to get married. My parents were delighted that I had finally renounced my bachelorhood—I was, after all, thirty-three, and they had begun to worry in earnest. But though they were pleased that I was about to become more respectable, they felt—I knew this with certainty—that my prospective wife carried with her three serious flaws that did not apply to Dorothy. The first was that she had just been divorced; the second and third were her two children. Was it for this I had waited all these years? A woman with two children? However unhappy, they maintained a steely resolve not to express any reservations about behavior they couldn't understand. And no one made a single unpleasant comment—until, that is, the day of the wedding.

July 1, 1970, was scorching hot, and my father had a thing about air conditioners—we had one, but he didn't like turn it on—and open windows; he preferred them closed. I melted through my batik tie and actually managed to stain my neck as the judge, my parents' friend, married us in their living room, exhorting the two of us to laugh our way through life's inevitable vicissitudes. After the ceremony, my friends Tony and Jon and I approached my father. Always exuberant, Tony blurted out, in a jolly mode, "Well, Dr. Rosenthal, what do you think of this?," meaning, obviously, What do you think of this lovely occasion in which Michael has finally gotten married?

"What, you mean this nightmare?" my father retorted.

Taken aback by an answer he hadn't anticipated, Tony stumbled over his words: "Dr. Rosenthal, you are usually so optimistic—what are you saying?"

"I usually am," my father replied, "but how can I be about something like this?"

The appalling nature of the formulation shocked me, though I immediately realized it had nothing to do with an evaluation of Judith and likely stemmed from his gut reaction to interpersonal complication of any sort, of which he was definitely not a fan. And whatever else one might say about this marriage, taking on two children did not speak to simplicity. Still, I could not be expected to celebrate hearing my generally reticent father burst out with "nightmare" several minutes after the judge had pronounced Judith and me wife and husband. Parents are entitled to their feelings, I would certainly maintain, though it is also fair to acknowledge that not all feelings need to be expressed.

The next night Judith's parents were taking us all to dinner and we were going to gather at my parents' apartment. I got there, by chance, before the others and was in the kitchen, filling up the ice bucket, when my father walked in. I had no intention of letting the opportunity pass. "I just want you to know I was tremendously embarrassed for you when you declared my marriage a nightmare yesterday," I told him.

"I didn't say that," he responded.

I bored in: "Well, you did. Tony heard you, Jon heard you, and I heard you. I can't forgive you."

He looked panicked and began clawing at my arm. "I didn't know what I was saying I . . . I must have been drunk," he muttered.

I was not about to let him get away with such a lame defense. "That's no excuse," I said, berating him, and then continued to attack, more pent-up anger than I knew I possessed bubbling to the surface.

In desperation, he concocted a brilliantly original gloss on his awful sentiment that immediately wrote itself into our family mythology: "I didn't mean anything pejorative by it." The notion of the non-pejorative nightmare, invoked in times of stress and urgency, has gotten Judith and me through many a difficult moment ever since.

FAMILY MATTERS

Despite these inauspicious beginnings, my parents, especially my mother, instantly bonded with Judith, recognizing the manifold virtues that had attracted me to her in the first place. The Sylvia-Judith relationship became a great source of pleasure for all of us. And when, two years later, we delivered the first—and last—Rosenthal grandson, on my father's very birthday, no less, the complications that had initially loomed so large in his eyes no longer seemed to matter.

And fifty-one years after that scorching July 1st, we are still happily laughing together.

Street Games

I have always resented accounts of New York's street sports that suggested that the only activity that really mattered to boys growing up in the city was stickball. Stories abound of serious athletes, like Joe Pepitone, the legendary Yankee first baseman, who could allegedly wallop the ball two (or was it three?) sewers' worth. Or Willie Mays, the Giants' unparalleled center fielder, who after a major league game at the Polo Grounds would occasionally stop off on his way home and share a few innings with the guys around the stadium. The implication was that if you didn't heft a broomstick, you must never have engaged in competitive games on New York streets.

At the risk of being condemned as a revisionist historian, I would like to make a claim, if not necessarily for the primacy of punchball in the rank order of urban entertainments, than at least for a recognition of its legitimate significance as a thoroughly absorbing pastime. I, for one, never swung a broomstick, but I punched a tennis ball with fervor when the older boys from 300 Central Park West assembled on Ninety-first Street for a game. We played more or less all the time when we weren't at school. I lived on the north side of Ninety-first Street, at 315. Though we inhabited a duplex, with my father's dermatological offices and our living room on the ground floor. I always felt vaguely embarrassed that my building was not nearly as grand as the two buildings on either side of ours and even lacked a pretentious name, which the other two possessed: the El Dorado, to the south, and the Ardsley, to the north. (My sensitivity on this score was weird but real. One evening when some adults who didn't know me were returning me by car from the suburbs and asked where I lived, I said Ninety-first and Central Park, and they stopped in front of the Ardsley, at 320, to let me out. I thanked them and walked through the Ardsley's front door—and then out the side door, reluctant to admit to strangers that I didn't live there.)

My active punchball career lasted about four years, roughly from when I was ten or so to fourteen. As the youngest kid in the game, I began as the smallest and arguably the worst. In the field, I was assigned to the outermost reaches, where I could do the least harm, as far down Ninety-first Street as was decent to position me. Stationed far away from home plate, located close to the Central Park West corner, I rarely had the opportunity to catch—or not to catch—the ball. But it was at bat (metaphorically speaking; no bat existed, of course) that my physical limitations were most glaringly apparent. With the fielders gathered contemptuously around the stoop serving as first base, I strove mightily to punch the ball over their heads, although generally, at least at the start, to little avail. Gradually, as I grew older and stronger, the contempt diminished, and I had to be defended the way the others were. It turned out I was actually quite skillful, more than capable of lacing line drives against the wall (the best place to hit them), counting on unpredictable bounces to elude the fielders.

Even as I improved the quality of my play over the years, however, my hitting technique remained quite primitive. Using my right arm as a club, hinged at the shoulder, I reared back, keeping the arm club straight, popped the ball into the air with my left, and smote it as hard as I could. If eventually I perfected the art of placing the ball beyond the reaches of the first baseman manning the stoop and against the wall of the building, I could never hit it very far. For that you needed to eschew the club for the power of the wrist.

The master of this style was Ira, the veritable Mickey Mantle or Barry Bonds of our block, who achieved a certain adult eminence as a poet, photographer, publisher, and filmmaker. But for me at the time, "the conscience of Planet Earth," as he went on to call himself, was simply the greatest punchball player of his era. Except when one of his scorching liners by chance ricocheted off the building into the hands of a fielder or got trapped behind one of the metal window guards on the first floor of our building—from which you would simply pluck it out without it touching the sidewalk—it was almost impossible to get him out. Unlike my somewhat stodgy, stiff-armed method, Ira's arm was bent at the elbow, his wrist held tightly next to his chest. Delivering maximum kinetic power with an efficient crack of the wrist, Ira sent the ball whizzing faster and farther than anybody else.

Unfortunately, at least from my perspective, just as I blossomed into my full teenage athletic glory, the older boys from 300 disappeared to colleges across the country, putting a permanent end to Ninety-first Street punchball. I was the last person left, and punchball was not a one-person game.

If Ira was unquestionably the greatest player of his generation, Irwin was arguably the oddest. Irwin refused, for reasons I never understood, to hit the ball in the air. He insisted on ground balls, either down the building side or, more insidiously, down the gutter side, where the cars were parked. If the ball passed the first-base stoop still on the sidewalk in fair territory and then took refuge under a car, it was declared a ground-rule double. Irwin held the all-time record for ground-rule doubles. He also held the all-time record (largely because no one else ever attempted it) for sliding on the pavement into second base to avoid a tag. In the process of trying to stretch one of his ground-ball singles into a double, he would hurl himself to the ground, indifferent to the possibility or even the inevitability of at least tearing his pants, if not the flesh from his legs. As long as he got to second safely, nothing else seemed to matter.

Ira and Irwin were the mainstays of our games. Lesser lights included Charlie, Lenny, Bobby, Alan (known as Bernie), Burton, and someone we called Junior, who lived not in the splendid El Dorado but somewhere down on Ninety-first Street and therefore, to my eyes, inhabited a slightly lower social class than the others. It was never discussed, but I felt the difference.

Of these second-echelon players, Bobby was the strangest. He was the only left-hander, which theoretically gave him the enormous advantage of having the best angle to place the ball, whenever he wanted, off the Ninety-first Street building, more or less guaranteeing him a hit. Despite this, and an elegant, languid overhand batting stroke, he almost always made an out, as he insisted on hitting the ball straight away as far as he could. Balls that landed in the street were deemed fouls, two fouls automatically constituted an out, and Bobby's majestic shots rarely came in contact with the sidewalk.

My career suffered under a serious handicap shared by no other player: the first-base stoop was actually the entrance of my father's medical office. Stumbling out the door after his ministrations, unwary patients ran the risk of being conked by one of Ira's ferocious drives, an act that would bring down paternal fury on the innocent but easily available object of his son. Even worse than hitting my father's patients, however, Ira's liners would occasionally exhibit the bad judgment of breaking one of his two office windows, which stood in our foul territory. At that point the game immediately ceased, as my father, demonstrating an athleticism I had never given him credit for, came whipping out of his door, shouting imprecations and scattering the players, who raced into the El Dorado, across the street, for safety. I, of course, could not escape and, as the others had fled, was required alone to endure his abuse. In time, new windows were installed, and games continued.

While punchball reigned as the king of activities on Ninety-first Street, it was by no means our only game. There was touch football, played with a tennis ball; roller-skating hockey, with a skate key as a puck; wall ball; stoopball; and Chinese handball. I never understood the notion that kids in the city didn't have places to play and things to do. We were at it on our street from morning to evening. And when there was nobody around and no competition, a wall, a ball, a baseball glove, and a bit of fantasy would do just fine. My singular animating fantasy had to do with being discovered by a major league baseball scout who would just happen to be passing by Ninety-first Street to witness the pinpoint accuracy of the blazing fastballs—if just tennis balls—I threw against the wall. This narrative of discovery stemmed from the career of Wilmer "Vinegar Bend" Mizell, a successful major league pitcher in the fifties and sixties who allegedly caught the eye of a scout while throwing rocks or baseballs or something against a barn as a young man in a small town in Alabama. If Vinegar Bend, I reasoned as I waited to be found, why not me? But no one came to observe how slowly I threw, and after several years of effort I had to accept that no one would.

Summer Camp

It is not clear to me how my mother (my father certainly wouldn't have been involved) determined that Green Mountain Camp in Vermont should constitute my initial summer experience away from home. As far as I know, there were no happy children of her friends who had enjoyed it; no underground document circulated among middle-class Jewish parents suggesting that if you wanted to get your kid out of the city for a couple of months, Green Mountain was the place for you.

I was eight, thoroughly untutored in the ways of the world, having never been away from my parents for any substantial amount of time. Previous summers had generally been spent in Schenectady, where my grandmother and uncle lived in a large house and he was a member of a nice country club. Uncle Paul maintained a garden in the back of the house, growing corn and tomatoes, which I was permitted to water and weed. I fed my pet squirrel, Pete, splashed around in the country club pool, enjoyed my comic books, and remained more or less perfectly content. But my mother understood that it would probably be a good idea to get me involved with boys my age and discover life on my own without her guidance. For whatever reason, Green Mountain was selected as the agency through which to achieve these admirable goals.

SCRAPS, ORTS, AND FRAGMENTS

Although I had no conception of what happened in summer camp, I was not opposed to going. I assume it must have been presented as an opportunity for all kinds of games, meeting new friends, learning to swim, and other assorted pleasurable experiences designed to entertain me. I could see nothing wrong with it. If I was perhaps a tad young to be taking on so much that was unfamiliar, with no emotional preparation for the mysteries and challenges of bunk living, even that didn't bother me. So in the summer of 1945, off I went to Camp Green Mountain.

From first minute to last, a total disaster. What I had no way of appreciating, and certainly my mother couldn't have known, was that in all male summer camps that took sports seriously, social success depended entirely on one's athletic competence. If you could throw a football, shoot a basketball, or hit a baseball, you were guaranteed popularity. If you fell short in these crucial areas, you were relegated to membership among those misfits deemed unworthy of anybody's friendship. This was the group to which I belonged. At that age, I could neither throw nor catch nor shoot nor run nor perform anything else that required grace or coordination. Given my inadequacies, I understood the lack of affection shown me by my bunkmates. Why would somebody care about someone as inept as I was? I hated my loneliness, but it seemed only appropriate.

While I felt I had to some extent earned my unhappiness by my manifold failures, I had difficulty accepting the conclusion that I should also be regularly beaten up for them. And yet I was. Not brutalized, of course, but punched around, thrown to the ground, arms twisted, and the like, all in service of demonstrating my inferiority. I didn't see why I should have to physically suffer, especially when, to my eight-year-old way of thinking, there were others more deserving of torment. In my bunk, for example, there was an even worse athlete—if possible—than me with a much worse name, which I still remember with clarity some seventy-seven years after: Willard Gellis. Not only did he have what I posited as a funny name, he wore glasses—two reasons why it made sense to me that he should be bullied. But with my normal name and no glasses, why me? We didn't come together in our shared plight, but I always felt that I should have been spared his treatment.

I don't remember having any fun or experiencing any pleasure throughout the summer except for one splendid moment. We were playing dodgeball, in which you throw a volleyball-sized ball at a person on the other team across a center line. If you hit him, he is out, but if he catches the ball, you, the thrower, are out. I was meandering around on my side as was my wont, not really paying attention to the flow of the game, my back to the opposing team. Suddenly I heard someone bark at me, "You're out" as I whirled around and in one motion caught the ball, which was just in the act of hitting me. It had been thrown by none other than Gary, the best athlete and the nastiest kid in my division. He was astonished, as was I. That I, the absolute dregs of my group, had succeeded in catching out the sublime Gary constituted some form of a miracle, a kind of violation of the natural order. How I managed to clutch the ball to my chest as it struck me I will never know, but I have never forgotten the sensation of my extraordinary accomplishment.

Only I could savor the magnitude of the catch, but insignificant as it was to the camping world at large, it provided the high point of my summer. For the rest, I was defined by my incompetence and misery. I knew enough not to admit my unhappiness by crying—which I never did. Instead, I maintained the fiction that everything was fine and declared that I couldn't wait for next summer to return to enjoy the splendors of Green Mountain.

Camp ended with an awards dinner designed to make the boys feel good about themselves and the skills they had mastered so that they might be encouraged to come back the next year. Every camper received a wooden plaque celebrating his achievements. A middling performance, for example, might include mention of swimming, track, baseball, volleyball, rowing. A superstar, like the transcendent Gary, would be cited for excellence in every conceivable athletic endeavor. As we ate our special last-night dessert of ice cream, a counselor read out the names of each camper and his successes. The recipient would then walk up to the dais amid scattered applause and receive the sacred plaque, testifying to a summer well spent.

What, I wondered, would they do with me, who had shown no aptitude for any of the manly arts? Then my name was called. Distinction in "nature and hiking," two of my most detested activities, was assigned to me, in lieu of there being anything else that I might have plausibly earned. The ridiculous and totally inappropriate award generated mild tittering among the assembled campers: the perfect humiliating conclusion to a dreadful summer.

Just as I refused to show weakness to my unfriendly bunkmates by revealing my unhappiness, so I determined not to admit to my parents how awful my eight weeks had been. I didn't complain, didn't discuss my lack of friends with them. So I don't remember how they concluded that I had been miserable, unless I was simply not as good at pretending as I thought. Whatever the reason, it was decided that I should not return to Green Mountain the following summer. Instead, a new destination was discovered by parental (maternal) investigation: Greylock, another sports-centric camp, this one in Becket, Massachusetts.

As the summer of 1946 approached, and without my being aware of it, I experienced a mysterious transformation. The god of coordination somehow chose to descend upon me, and in place of the pathetic creature who had elicited the laughter of his peers for his achievements in nature and hiking emerged someone who could throw, catch, and hit. I remained a lousy swimmer, but that hardly mattered. Land-game skills were what counted, and I had suddenly become among the best. I gobbled up grounders hit to me by counselors, threw the ball farther than anyone else, hit home runs, and even made an unassisted triple play in a game. By the ineluctable law of summer camp dynamics, my newly discovered athletic gifts guaranteed my popularity, People sought me out. I even exacted revenge for having been bullied at Green Mountain by turning into a bit of a bully myself, establishing a club in which membership was earned by being hit by me with a hairbrush until you cried. There were no other benefits. Boys lined up to join. Fortunately, I closed it down after a short while. At Greylock's version of Green Mountain's ceremonial final awards dinner, at which only the best at every sport was honored, I erased what I considered the stain of being celebrated for excellence in nature and hiking by winning the baseball cup for my age group. I had come a long way in a year.

I loved Greylock and couldn't wait to go back every year. Each summer, of course, was exactly like the last, which is why I was so happy. No such thing as growth or change in a successful eight-week summer camp. Just more of the same. In my case, sports were all that mattered, and I played every game with passion and some degree of proficiency. Over the next four years, if I never quite scaled the mountain of winning the award for best all-around athlete, I was invariably one of the several runners-up, which was fine for me.

Although founding and implementing my exclusive pain-infliction beating club surely marked my moral low point at camp, I did also experience, at least in my own mind, a memorable, if slightly bizarre, morally transcendent moment. It occurred a year or two later and involved our bunk counselor, an odd fellow named Ben whom no one especially liked. One morning before breakfast, Ben summoned the six or seven of us in the bunk together and hinted darkly that the evening before, after we had gone to bed, he had witnessed some unacceptable behavior that he didn't want repeated. He refused to be specific as to what he had observed, or whom he had seen engaging in it, but he was putting us on notice there was to be no more of it.

Having no idea what had happened, we immediately began our own cross-examination of one another to determine guilt, innocence, and the nature of the transgression. While our feverish investigation over the next few days produced no evidence about anything, somewhere along the line the notion of something known as "masturbation" found its way into the discussion, probably inserted by Ben himself.

This was all I needed to ignite my moral outrage. As the son of the assistant commissioner of health in New York, who was never big about talking to me, certainly about sexual matters, I would frequently find public health flyers, English on one side, Spanish on the other, lying around the apartment, presumably intended for me to learn about health issues of various sorts that my father might otherwise find awkward to raise with me. It was from one of these documents that I read about the naturalness of masturbation, the importance of accepting it as normal. The one problem with the information dispensed by this literature was its complete failure to explain what the act consisted of, so that while I knew that neither shame nor regret could properly be attached to it, I didn't have the vaguest idea what it was.

Nevertheless, when I began to realize that perhaps it was masturbation that Ben claimed to have witnessed, I became incensed. "There's nothing wrong with it," I bellowed at the hapless counselor.

SUMMER CAMP

"It's people like you who make it out to be bad." And on and on I went, savaging poor Ben, who must have been aghast at the torrent of self-righteous abuse I directed at him. Fortunately for me, he remained totally unaware that my fervor coexisted with total ignorance. Whether he had actually seen anything or was simply acting as a provocative sicko—as I suspect was probably the case—my rage put an end to the whole business, terminating accusations and investigations alike. And Ben got his tip at the end of the summer, just like all the other counselors.

I returned as a happy Greylock camper for the next few years, until my mother finally convinced me there were other possibilities I might consider. Reluctant as I was to change the pleasantly familiar for the unknown, nevertheless I agreed, and departed at fourteen to Putney work camp in Vermont and an entirely different kind of experience. Instead of playing sports, one actually worked—in the garden, the kitchen, the barn, on the roads. In addition to replacing sports with work, Putney offered an even more potent brew of reality: a coeducational environment. Having attended Greylock and the Horace Mann School, two all-male institutions, I was now for the first time living in the presence of girls. A revelation, if a little late. While I realize that eventually I would have figured out how to talk to them, Putney was the place where I initially learned. It was also the place where I succeeded in exchanging my first kiss—accompanied by a ferocious migraine headache, which, on balance, seemed a price worth paying. I don't know what my mother imagined would occur during my first coed summer, but kudos to her for getting me started on something approximating real life.

Hubert's

Almost no one objected to the cleaning up of New York's Time Square some years ago. Everyone seemed to agree that ridding the city of the sleazy and the noxious—the pornographic movie theaters, inhabited by the iconic dirty old men with their loathsome masturbatory habits, the sex shops with their filthy magazines and who knows what kinds of illicit activities in the back—made New York a more salubrious, safer place. Forty-second Street is demonstrably a nicer, kinder destination without the squalor. Tourists can happily attend live theater, the credulous can be amazed at the delights in Ripley's Believe it or Not, you can catch a glimpse of Elizabeth Taylor, Marilyn Monroe, and maybe even Winston Churchill or the Pope in Madame Tussaud's wax museum.

But if the transformation of the neighborhood should properly be endorsed, I confess that I have only the finest memories of the splendidly tawdry Hubert's flea circus, located on the south side of Forty-second Street, not far from Eighth Avenue, in a building designed by the distinguished architect Stanford White. During my high school years, in the early fifties, it provided me with a titillating refuge from my buttoned-up, suffocatingly proper middle-class existence. Just a local subway ride away, Hubert's was a site of oddity, mystery, dusky sensuality. Exactly what the perfervid imagination of a fourteen-year-old boy required. I loved it.

Hubert's consisted of two floors. The street level, open to all at no charge, was what we called then a "penny arcade" or "shooting gallery," filled with games of chance and skill: shooting bears with a light beam as they rushed across the screen, causing them to rear up, growl, and move in the other direction; torpedoing bucktoothed Japanese sailors from a submarine while your tonnage sunk got recorded in the upper right-hand corner of the machine; shooting down German bombers with accurate anti-aircraft guns; determining your sex appeal by seeing how tightly you could grip the two prongs of a resistant handle; attempting to roll a ball up an inclined plane into the highest numbered hole; and, perhaps best of all, playing countless games on numerous old-fashioned pinball machines complete with flashing lights and flippers. On the occasions when I went there with several friends, we would crowd into a narrow booth and amuse ourselves mightily by shouting, until the recording disk ran out, "Viva Zapata!," the movie starring Marlon Brando, which we saw endlessly. As I think back about it now, there was absolutely nothing funny whatsoever in what we were doing, but we thought it extraordinarily hilarious then.

The first floor, in short, offered sufficient entertainments to occupy us happily for hours. It was varied and absorbing, but it didn't speak to the deeper satisfactions. You could tell because there was an admission fee to get downstairs. Was it .75 cents or $1.25? I can't remember. However exorbitant, it was well worth it (keep in mind that as a teenager with a small allowance in the 1950s, my resources were limited), at least for me. That's where the action was, that's where the eponymous fleas were, when they were in fact present, which was by no means on every visit. The absence of the fleas didn't bother me, as the fleas themselves, fascinating as they were, never accounted for Hubert's prime appeal, even if they were its most distinctive feature.

Describing the achievements of the talented fleas to largely skeptical listeners since then has never been an easy task. The assumption, as I explain having witnessed them kicking tiny footballs, pulling minuscule chariots, or racing against each other, is that I am either hallucinating or deliberately lying, and it is almost impossible to dislodge. No way, or so the argument runs, could frail, hapless fleas possibly do such things, never mind traversing a teeny high wire (well, not *that* high, of course). You don't have to necessarily be a flea lover to find it depressing how little faith people are willing to invest in the capacity of fleas to perform feats of strength and balance.

Despite the general refusal to accept the credibility of my testimony regarding flea prowess, I have continued, over the past seventy years or so, to maintain the accuracy of everything I reported. I admit that in my weaker moments I began to think that perhaps I had been tricked into imagining what could not possibly be, but finally I could not bring myself to reject the evidence of my senses. I *had* seen them doing what people denied they could do: it was fact, not fake news or a hoax.

After decades of nagging uncertainty, at last, confirmation. It no longer mattered if no one believed me, for now I had proof that I had been right all along. It came last year in the person of my good friend Richard, whom I was visiting at his home in Santa Fe. In the midst of our reminiscing about growing up in New York, he casually dropped the remark that he had gone several times to Hubert's. I couldn't believe my luck. I had never thought of Richard and Hubert's in the same breath. He confirmed the exploits I remembered. He, too, had been amazed. Both of us together couldn't be wrong. Let the doubters doubt. I could now tell the story of Hubert's fleas to my grandchildren with confidence.

After descending the stairway and ponying up the tariff, one came into a large, basement-like space with an elevated stage, on which various of Hubert's acts would take place. The cohort of those who had ventured down the stairs to be entertained was, of course, almost entirely male, sometimes with a female in tow, and largely middle-aged. They were clearly spontaneous walk-ins, not people who had purposely set out, as I had, for an exotic adventure. I was invariably the youngest.

In my view, there were essentially two classes of performers at Hubert's: the innocuous and the compelling. The innocuous included the likes of the elephant lady, who long before tattoos were de rigueur was more or less totally tattooed and would flaunt her decorated self before the gawking public, encouraging the barker who presided over the display to claim she possessed a form of elephant skin; a man with two deformed arms who would place a rifle of some sort over his shoulder and, standing fifteen yards away with his back to a candle, look into a mirror and shoot out the flame; a faux Indian fakir, jumping up and down and lying on a bed of nails; Olga, the bearded lady, sporting a lush beard; a sword swallower; a snake dancer, said to be an African princess; and a midget lady, among others.

These had their attractions, to be sure, but hardly enough to encourage the return to Forty-second Street of an experience-starved adolescent in search of something—anything—not generally available on the Upper West Side. What kept me coming back was less the superbly trained fleas than the bizarre Albert-Alberta, whose strangeness I always found riveting. Looking like some old drag queen wreathed in a blousy, loose-fitting gown, Albert-Alberta projected a unique bodily identity, half man, half woman, neatly divided vertically down the middle. "I was born in *la belle France*," he would begin in an indistinguishable foreign accent, "of a normal mothere and a normal fathere." An ordinary French teenage girl, until she began to turn into an ordinary French teenage boy. No reasons, hormonal, genetic, or otherwise, given. It just happened, and from then on, he was simultaneously man and woman. At Hubert's he advertised his duality with some drama: "My left breast is the breast of a woman," he sharply announced, opening his gown to reveal the contours of a luxurious breast. "My right breast is the breast of a man," he indicated, permitting us to see a muscular chest. He then parted his gown to demonstrate the two different qualities of leg, a delicate female and a robust male. Was it an illusion shaped by talented makeup artists? A biological anomaly? I could never quite resolve how they did it or if they did it, but I was always fascinated. "I have pictures of things you want to see as naked as the palm of my hand," he would intone at the end of his performance, drawing a finger suggestively on his palm, though that would cost a little extra.

The enigma that was Albert-Alberta had nothing to do with the simple masculinity of Sailor Jim the Strongman, who generally came next. If, as I realize now, Albert-Alberta was culturally ahead of his time, playing with notions of gender fluidity and the like, Sailor Jim offered no such complexity. Encased in a leopard-skin toga, flabby muscles showing around the edges, Jim engaged in displays of power, lifting, pushing, pulling. Were the steel bars he squeezed in half really steel? Who knows: I went to Hubert's for intrigue, never expecting clarity. Jim's singular achievement involved placing a large spike in a metal holder and firmly gripping it with his gums, bend it toward him. On one occasion the spectacle of a sixtyish man in a toga with his chops around a spike bearing down with all his weight proved too much for my friend Steve and me and we began to laugh. If we weren't witnessing high art, Jim still obviously felt entitled to respectful attention, and he was—understandably—seriously offended. But revenge was at hand. After Jim finished demonstrating his bending skills, he would walk to the front of an enclosed structure—really, I guess, a small room—and sell tickets for Laura the dancing girl.

It cost an additional quarter to see Laura, but when Steve attempted to pay, Jim glowered at him, pronounced him too young for such forbidden sights, and turned him away. Thankfully, even though I too had been guilty of laughter, Jim permitted me in.

Crowding into the small space in the expectation of confronting a scantily clad or even—was it possible?—an entirely unclad female represented the fantasy high point of the Hubert visit. Having spent endless hours with friends speculating on the mysteries and organization of a naked woman's body, I found the thought of perhaps actually managing a glimpse of one nothing short of a divine gift. And yet, or so the hope went, maybe, just maybe this time . . .

Needless to say, no luck. The lights went out, the creaky phonograph started up, and the divine Laura suddenly began to rise slinkily out of a bathtub onstage, shrouded in what appeared to be a thoroughly opaque shower curtain. She moved her hands seductively up and down her arms and legs and around her body, providing illumination with small bulbs worn between her fingers. After several minutes of watching her glide around but seeing absolutely nothing of what I hungered for, I had to accept that my quest for primal knowledge had once again been foiled. Laura disappeared, the lights were turned on, and we all filed out, none the wiser or more satisfied for the experience.

Although the show had ended, Hubert's had no intention of letting us escape without making one last effort to squeeze out a few more cents. For another—and final—75 cents, you could purchase a sexual goody bag, which allegedly included naked photographs of assorted performers, like the elephant lady and the midget lady, and a pair of "Chinese handcuffs"—a compressible paper tube into which, as the barker suggested, you invite your girlfriend to place a finger of each hand before beginning to molest her. As she tries to pull away, the tube tightens around her two fingers, locking her in: handy for seduction.

But the prize item available for the shrewd purchaser was a small, innocent-looking box with some extraordinary properties. Invented, we were told, during World War II, to help plane spotters identify enemy aircraft, it enabled people to look into it and, through a clever arrangement of mirrors, see the underbellies of planes flying overhead. In peacetime, however, a marvelous new use for this box had been found. Instead of seeing the markings of planes flying high in the sky, the box would invert the images of women walking on the street and offer an unhindered view up their dresses. No more crick in the neck hiding under the boardwalk, our pitchman emphasized; just employ our little box and women would without knowing it be flipped upside down for your scrutiny.

A superb fantasy, if somewhat loony. Not only would the women be inverted, but their dresses would fall over in the process. It was difficult to buy into this one, and I never capitulated. I did, however, follow one buyer out of Hubert's. He opened his bag on the street, put the box to his eye, and promptly threw it away. I picked it up and looked in. Like so much else about my encounter at Hubert's, it was empty.

Sex in the Fifties for Nice Horace Mann Boys

The overarching concern for me and my group of friends during the early fifties was whether or not we would die as virgins. We worried about it, talked about it endlessly, dreamt majestic dreams of fulfillment. The smart money strongly favored death before satisfaction.

For one thing, as prisoners of an all-boys school and an all-male summer camp, most of us didn't know any girls, certainly any girls who might do *that*, which limited any solution. Even if we did discover girls similarly interested and willing, we remained so lamentably ignorant about the mysteries of the female body that we almost certainly couldn't have managed without on-site tutorial help. We argued at length over the location of apertures and how one navigated them. We brought yellow pads and pencils to our discussions, drawing our own idiosyncratic road maps on stick figures to explain to each other what we should be seeking. Rumor had reached us about something called the clitoris, for example. Where was it? What was it? How was it pronounced? (Accent falling on the first or second syllable?) What should we do if we happened to bump into one? Conversations could be heated. In one especially contentious session, Steve claimed that his mother had insisted that the complications of intercourse were such that his parents had had to go to the doctor's office to be set up in the proper position. This sounded wrong to me, and I protested violently. But what did I know? Maybe that was the way the adult world worked, though I doubted this. Surely a presumably pleasurable act couldn't be that difficult to manage. No consensus was reached.

We hungered for glimpses of the real thing. While nudist magazines, containing jolly photographs of naked volleyball games on the beach, were for sale at select stores, they failed even to begin to satisfy because of the ban on displaying pubic hair. Apparently the protectors of public morality felt that a sighting of hair was too much for the adolescent imagination to handle, so none was available. Breasts were fine, but that was all. Occasionally a pornographic playing card, more valuable than bitcoin, would surface in the Horace Mann locker room, featuring a smiling woman with legs akimbo, complete with the prohibited, sought-after presence of hair. How we would gather round, pushing and shoving, to cop a glimpse of the sacred parts.

Although we remained firmly in the grip of the sexual drought as we moved into our sophomore and junior years, we began to stumble into awkward, joyless dating: terrible school dances, featuring Lester Lanin beanies and doing the bunny hop, painful parties in which we struggled to make conversation with girls we didn't know and who seemed not the least interested in us. From time to time reports drifted back from our more intrepid colleagues about heroic exploits undertaken on the sexual front lines. I once overheard on the morning subway to school a Fieldston girl telling her friend that she had "washed her mouth out afterward," and I almost swooned at the thought of what must have happened. Entombed in frustration and racked with craving, we invented pathetic categories of sexual achievement by which we could rate our progress and earn the respect of friends. The most rudimentary level, but one that nevertheless conferred credit, was called "getting covered breast," which could be invoked if your hand made contact, no matter how fleeting or accidental, with the clothed female breast. This didn't count a lot, but it still counted. Learned scholars of our sexual struggles would debate at length whether touching the outside of the breast with the inside of the hand should be judged of greater value than a casual encounter with the back of the hand. It was generally agreed that you could claim success in either case, though fingers and palm, speaking obviously to conscious intent, necessarily carried a higher value.

The next stage on the trajectory of sexual accomplishment, working in from the dress or blouse, was "getting covered brassiere." No question of the significance of this undertaking, as it frequently involved unbuttoning and unzipping, skills we hadn't mastered, not to speak of sometimes complicated angles of hand insertion. But to feel the skimpy material beneath the outer layer of clothing and to know than an actual breast lurked within generated almost more titillation than one could stand.

Since no one I knew had the daring or confidence to attempt to explore below the waist, encountering the unencumbered breast, should access be granted to it, represented the most exalted form of sexual aspiration, the "holy of holies," to which all—or at least a great deal—of human striving was directed. Known on the street as "getting bare tit," it provided us with the stuff of masturbatory fantasies and much self-congratulation. As for the pawing and groping our dates had to endure while we fumbled our way in search of a breast, we can only honor them for their toughness and resilience. Certainly extending pleasure to another human being occupied none of our overheated imaginations. We were busy "scoring" and "getting," creating narratives of our conquests, such as they were, for later rehashing with our buddies. No one worried about what the girls might be feeling.

But it was becoming clear that none of our efforts, however successful, were destined to resolve the race we felt we were running against death. To rid ourselves of the burden of virginity would obviously require a new approach: professional intervention. To this end, clusters of friends set out to find the timely phone number that would release us, under congenial, non-scary circumstances, from our enforced innocence.

With the number not forthcoming, a group of us had gathered at Eighty-sixth Street and Broadway on a fall Saturday afternoon to choose a movie. Most wanted the double feature at the RKO Eighty-first. I preferred Loews Eighty-third. When no one chose to accompany me, I went off by myself. So I was unaware that the Eighty-first Street contingent had somehow obtained the timely number after their movies had ended and made arrangements for a mass indoctrination into adulthood. Unfortunately, detectives were also interested in what was, after all, an illegal activity, and instead of liberation being achieved, my friends were required to testify in court as to the specific illicit services they were slated to receive. Threatened with "things being put on the record," fatally damaging their college hopes if they refused to cooperate, the four or five of them all admitted to what they'd had in mind. No consequences followed for them, but the intrusion of the law into our aspirations cast a pall on everyone's hopes. Although my taste in movies had spared me the embarrassment of the others, I shared their pain and disappointment. And our predicament remained unsolved.

But now my friend Norman, who had been one of the Eighty-first Street group, decided it was time for more aggressive action. Within a month, working from different sources, he came up with a new number. Was I in with him? he wanted to know. "Ready to go," I assured him, attempting to project a cheery enthusiasm I didn't in the least feel. "Make the arrangements."

Several weeks later, the dreaded call came: I was to report to Norman's Central Park West apartment early on Saturday evening for a briefing. When I arrived, we confronted our shared terror together. Neither of us had ever tasted Scotch before, but we both agreed that a tiny snort might be helpful in addressing our anxiety. We indulged. It didn't help. The explanation of the plans, to my mind, significantly enhanced the necessity of the Scotch. According to Norman, we were to enter a particular SRO building in the West Eighties (I forget the exact address) at approximately seven-thirty, find the fifth-floor bathroom, go inside, sit down (edge of the bathtub? toilet?), and wait for a woman to summon us, one at a time. This made no sense to me. Why wouldn't we knock on her door? What was the point of stashing us in the bathroom? "Norman," I pleaded, "this can't be right." He had no convincing retort, other than that these were the instructions he had received and we had to follow them. With my skepticism matched only by my fear, I realized that I had no choice if I wanted to ascend to sexual adulthood. Bizarre it might be, but I marched off with Norman.

Twenty minutes or so later, I found myself sitting in a dilapidated bathroom on the edge of the bathtub, having conceded the more comfortable toilet to Norman in honor of his achievement in getting us there. But there was no comfort to be had. We both began to sweat profusely. No one spoke. The sound of our heavy breathing mingled with some low-grade moaning. Every now and then we would hear footsteps in the hall, doors opening, bits of murmured conversation. The inviting knock on the door, summoning us from our voluntary bathroom incarceration to fulfillment, however, never came. Norman was in no state to be criticized, so I limited myself to casting beseeching, quizzical glances at him, as if he had some magical power to make things happen. At some level, of course, I was gratified that nothing was happening, though I knew I couldn't admit to such views.

Finally, after an hour of immobile, sweaty anxiety, Norman had to agree that being stuck in a fifth-floor bathroom did not constitute the first stage on the path to the sexual indoctrination we sought. Rather, a grim dead end. As he had clearly screwed up, he understood that he would have to address the confusion without my help. I was not about to venture out of what had by now become the security of the bathroom to discover what had gone wrong. He was not happy about his solitary mission, but he went manfully to the designated apartment to inquire about our alleged appointment. Several minutes later, he returned with some not very satisfying explanation about misunderstanding the arrangement. In any case, it was now too late. We were required to leave the building as pure as when we'd entered. I didn't press him about his culpability, even if I was confident that prostitutes are probably quite competent in organizing their schedules. At least I didn't have to sit any longer on the tub.

As we waited for the elevator, a customer lucky enough to have had access to the services denied us came into the hall. The elevator arrived and the three of us got in. I stared at my feet, thinking it appropriate to allow the client his privacy. Norman had a different sense of protocol. "How was she?" he suddenly barked, as if he would know good from bad. Somehow I managed to refrain from laughing hysterically at Norman's display of faux macho. "I've had worse," the gentleman responded in tough-guy kind, putting the seal of absurdity on the evening. The best part of the adventure was the hamburger we treated ourselves to as a reward for our courage.

With the initial disaster of the detectives' intervention followed by Norman's bungling, we more or less gave up on the notion that we could solve our problem though want ads. Although it seemed odd that in the entire city of New York we could find no way to satisfy our needs, the facts were indisputable: we had tried and failed. No one had the stomach for continued commercial searches, and we returned to the round of awkward dances and dreadful parties, leavened with the fruitless pullings and tuggings on living room sofas that had defined our previous amateur (and amateurish) efforts. Besides, we had entered our senior year of high school, and college panic had driven out most other forms of anxiety. If death were to carry us away before we experienced the joys of intercourse, so be it—as long as we got into our first-choice schools. This was, after all, Horace Mann, and we had our priorities straight.

There is no doubt that none of my Horace Mann friends had shed their virginity by graduation. I, for one, still didn't really know any girls. The night of our senior prom, for example, I went with my friend Jon to see Clark Gable in *Gone with the Wind*. Much more fun than obligatory dancing, I thought.

Freshman year at Harvard was as sexually arid as all my high school years. It wasn't until that summer that Rodney, a student I had met at college who was spending the vacation in New York, came up with a number that worked: it led me to Frances, in a ground-floor brownstone in the West Seventies. My nervousness was no less great than when I was stuck on the tub with Norman, but I was determined to see it through and rid myself of the scourge of my ignorance. And so I did. It took all of ten seconds, maybe less, marked by my success in putting on the condom before exploding. The television set remained on and Frances coughed a lot. I don't remember any pleasure associated with the act other than relief that I had beaten the grim reaper to the finish line.

The Choice

It happened sixty-seven years ago, and it would be difficult to imagine a more insignificant piece of a life over which to obsess. So how can it be that at age eighty-three, I still think about it, still cannot understand what was going through my head, still wonder how I could have been so stupid. If it had involved something substantial with real consequences, like what I planned to do with myself or what school I wanted to attend or whom I would marry (or not) or whether I should join the army, I could appreciate why I might dwell on the moment. But it had none of that resonance. Instead it concerned my decision to skip three days of freshman basketball practice at Harvard in order to finish an essay for my section of Humanities 4: Good and Evil in the Western World, on the meaning of Beatrice in Dante's *Divine Comedy*. A combination of theology and divine revelation, I finally determined.

To understand the issue it is necessary first to ask what a skinny Jew from New York who could neither run fast nor jump high was doing as a starter on the freshman basketball team. Although I'd nurtured dreams of playing college basketball while in high school, I'd doubted that I could achieve them. My varsity coach at Horace Mann

School never approved of me, much preferring—understandably, I guess—his son, who was two years younger, considerably shorter, and, without any question, totally incompetent as a player. "Rosenthal," Coach Miller once snapped at me, "if you ever decide to make some baskets I will give you a bouquet of flowers."

Despite his lack of regard for my offensive skills, I did possess a number of them. It was still the era of the two-handed set shot, and I had developed an absolutely deadly one, a scoring threat from anywhere on the court. (If only the three-point line existed then, there is no telling what I might have managed.) In addition, I loved playing defense and had become an implacable defender, considering it a personal affront when the man I was guarding happened to score. Perhaps most important, I had mastered the art of the crossover dribble, taught to me by my JV coach, "Mickey" Corcoran, a man who went on to fame and even a tiny bit of fortune as the high school basketball coach and later friend and mentor of the legendary professional football coach Bill Parcells. Practiced today by every five- and six-year-old playing with a basketball, it was a technique of crisply changing the direction of your dribble, essentially unknown in the early 1950s. Armed with this you could avoid even the staunchest defenders, leaving them tripping over themselves while you made your way to the basket. As I declared at the fiftieth reunion of my high school class, it was the most valuable lesson I ever learned at Horace Mann.

With my undistinguished career firmly behind me, I embarked for Cambridge in the fall of 1954, assuming my competitive basketball playing days were over. It seemed presumptuous to imagine that being on the varsity team in a school with ninety seniors would prepare me to make the team in a class of one thousand freshmen drawn from all over the country. Observing around me, in the early weeks of college, some tall, athletic-looking people and listening to their talk, while standing on registration lines, about winning state championships, performing thunderous dunks, and other noteworthy exploits confirmed my sense that basketball was now for entertainment only. Besides, one went to college to study, not to play.

So pickup games in the gym for exercise appeared to be the conclusion of my love of basketball. But then a peculiar thing happened. I began to notice that the celebrators of thunderous dunks proved slightly leaden-footed, that the state champions had difficulty dribbling with their left hands, and that no one could figure out how I left them behind as I mysteriously glided past with my crossover maneuver. They might be bigger, stronger and certainly more confident (and louder), but they were arguably not better. I decided to go out for the team. By the time tryouts opened, several months later, I had determined both that I deserved to be on the squad and that I was, according to my own hard-nosed estimate, the best guard candidate.

It turned out that the coach agreed with my privately held self-assessment, and in short order I found myself not only on the team but starting. A thoroughly unimaginable goal, difficult to digest. On the one hand, it struck me as impossible; on the other, totally appropriate, as I had legitimately earned my position by dint of serious, successful effort. I understood the game, courtesy of Mr. Corcoran, played good defense, knew what I was doing. I even had what I called my Irwin Shaw experience to help convince me that I belonged. Shaw's short story "The Eighty-Yard Run" opens with Christian Darling, a football player of indifferent abilities, at an unnamed university somewhere in the Midwest, leaping to catch a pass. Grabbing it away from the defender, he slips tackles, fakes out approaching defensive backs, straight-arms the safety, and strides into the end zone for an elegant eighty-yard touchdown run. His finest moment as an athlete, admired by all who were watching, suggesting the great things in store for him. Then the coach blows the whistle and we understand that we were witnessing not a game but only a late-afternoon practice that included his singular triumph, never to be repeated in actual competition.

My cherished eighty-yard run occurred during our first preseason scrimmage against the varsity. We were as close to a disorganized rabble as it was possible to be, having just come together as a team, everyone still in the process of learning everybody else's name. Playing against the varsity, under the scrutiny of the varsity coach, was not designed to calm the nerves, and for the first half of the scrimmage we were mostly intent on trying to avoid errors rather than do anything notably positive. I don't remember taking a shot in the first half, for example, anxious lest I miss it.

At halftime our coach, recognizing that we were performing well below our level of competence, urged us to relax, play the way we were capable of playing, shoot if we were free, and stop worrying about failure. Easier said than done, of course, but I decided to take his instructions to heart. I was guarding, and being guarded by the Harvard captain. When the second half began, I came down the court, received the ball, noticed the captain giving me a little room, and decided to do what I had refrained from doing thus far: shoot from outside. As I mentioned earlier, I was quite proficient at this. The shot settling neatly in the basket loosened me up considerably. A few minutes later, I found myself in a similar situation, and did not hesitate to shoot again. The same result: *swish*. Now I felt like Christian Darling, certain I couldn't be stopped. Some seconds later, another opportunity presented itself. And now the moment: "Don't let him shoot," I heard the coach roar, but he was too late. Up it went, and in it went. Three for three. Against the varsity captain.

Observed by the varsity coach, exhorting his captain to attempt to shut me down. What more could I have wanted? Nothing. Absolutely nothing. Never mind that it was merely a scrimmage and that the coach paid no attention to me afterward. I had caught his attention, if only fleetingly, a feat that would remain with me forever.

Our freshmen coach was a nice man whose qualifications for the job were that he was the head coach for the varsity soccer and lacrosse teams. As far as I could tell, he knew nothing about basketball. When the previous year's freshmen coach—he who had yelled to prevent me from shooting—had been promoted to lead the varsity, Harvard, notoriously uninterested in basketball at that time, had looked around for an inexpensive solution to direct the freshmen program. They found Mr. Munro, whose two sport affiliations undoubtedly meant he was familiar with the science of coaching—assuming there is such a thing—but did not necessarily suggest that he possessed any knowledge regarding the actual game of basketball. No one cared that he had few ideas to impart to us about what we were doing wrong or how we could get better. We practiced dutifully and I continued to play well, so much so that Coach Munro actually named me captain for our first game, before the team had a chance to vote. There was no way in 1954 that an ironic Jew from New York would survive a team vote for captain, and when eventually we all voted, an entirely inoffensive, tall person from the Midwest won. Still, the coach's appointing me constituted another highly improbable recognition I had never expected to earn.

While the last year's freshmen team had been undefeated, we started our season as if we might never win a game. We lost our first three, a consequence of the coach using the wrong players (not me, of course) and inadequate preparation. He had not bothered, for example, to have us practice what we might do if, ahead near the end, the other team decided to apply full-court defensive pressure. Sure enough, leading by ten points throughout most of our first game, we totally collapsed when we were pressed and managed to give away what should have been an easy victory. We really deserved a proper basketball coach rather than an experienced soccer and lacrosse coach. It was too bad that Harvard didn't feel it could afford one.

Finally, in our last game before Christmas break, we beat Providence. We were all excited to win, and I thought I had been particularly effective, scoring a dozen points, stealing the ball numerous times, and playing an intelligent floor game. The only problem with this judgment, though I didn't realize it at the time, was its role in convincing me of my importance to the team. Obviously, or so I imagined, it couldn't get along without me.

Harvard had a peculiar academic calendar during the fifties that called for two weeks of classes and final exams after Christmas vacation, rather than terminating the semester with the holiday. So when I left Cambridge for New York, I knew there would be work to be submitted shortly upon returning. It is not easy to focus on Dante when the city is bedecked in Christmas finery and endless festivities, family and otherwise, abound. Despite my best efforts, which even included taking refuge in the reading room of the public library for several days, I could not pull together my thoughts on what Beatrice represented. Back I went to Harvard, with a blank yellow pad and a heart filled with panic.

What to do about my unwritten paper? Classes in the mornings and practice in the afternoons would leave little time for fashioning profound insights about Beatrice. I felt trapped and more than slightly hysterical. Options like asking the instructor for an extension or even handing the paper in late didn't occur to me. I could only focus on liberating my afternoons from practice so I could ponder the complexities of Dante.

SCRAPS, ORTS, AND FRAGMENTS

From the perspective of sixty-seven years later, it astonishes me that I could have been so overwhelmed by something as trivial as the prospect of a late paper. But I suppose one does not possess the wisdom at seventeen that one presumably does at eighty-three. Not unlike Dante, I could not see my way out of the dark wood of confusion. Virgil didn't appear accessible for a conversation to help set me straight—whatever straight might be—nor, for that matter, did Beatrice. And I never even bothered to consult my roommates, lesser sources of moral authority. No, I stood alone, groping for the right path.

How I came to choose the worst possible solution remains a mystery. I had never missed a day of practice in my life, and surely I knew that no coach would look kindly on a player who exhibited such a lack of concern for his team as to simply not show up for a couple of days. What could I possibly have been thinking that would lead me to cavalierly throw away the significant achievement—which actually meant a great deal to me—of having made myself into the starting guard on the Harvard freshman team? If there is no answer that is wholly satisfactory, there are at least fragments of the case I can remember.

The first is what I have come to understand as the bogus, highfalutin intellectual argument: I came to Harvard not to play basketball but to be a student. In any conflict in priorities, the academic ones must necessarily take precedence. If missing practice to work on my Dante paper results in losing my position on the team, so be it. Although this situated me firmly, in my own eyes at least, on the moral high ground, it strikes me now as feeble. While finding the time to write a paper is a defensible good, so is playing for your school. Not a matter of one or the other. A sensible person must be able to discover a way, under stress, to do both. I couldn't.

THE CHOICE

A derivative of the insistence that basketball is less important than Dante was my realization that basketball was in any case not forever—or even necessarily for much longer. Could my modest abilities have gotten me to the varsity level? Possibly, but I harbored no illusions that I was destined for athletic greatness. And if playing for the freshmen represented the highest mountain I could climb, then it followed logically that jeopardizing my status by skipping practice could not be construed as so terrible. What, after all, was I actually giving up?

The third—and most shameful—part of the brief for devoting the next few afternoons to the library and not the court had to do with the exaggerated sense of my own value I had come to entertain. Since I had done so well against Providence, demonstrating that I was indeed the best guard, surely the coach could not afford to lose me. He would understand and approve my academic seriousness; there would be no long-term consequences. I wasn't, after all, goofing off. The notion that as a teammate I might owe some commitment to the others never occurred to me. It was only about me and my predicament.

Opposed to this tripartite case for toiling on Dante remained the simple fact that being a starting member of the basketball team constituted something worthwhile in which I could take legitimate pride and should have done everything in my power to preserve. I liked the game. I liked my success. I even enjoyed, I must admit, the low-grade distinction playing on the team conferred upon me among my classmates. Whether or not I moved to the next level, I had created something, in an admittedly small universe, quite extraordinary. How could I have been so casual about it? Why would I be willing to put it all at risk? If I could have spoken to my mature self with a broad perspective who over the years guided many Columbia students to find their way, I suspect I would have come up with a different answer. "Of course go to practice," I would have told me. "Starting on the freshmen team is a rare opportunity—after all, only five people manage it—and it will provide you with wonderful memories not found in discussion sections about *The Divine Comedy*. Ask for an extension. Enjoy what you have achieved for yourself. And who knows, maybe you could make it to the varsity." Unfortunately, that self was not around for advice. There was only the frantic soul who had gained admission to Harvard not for his basketball prowess but because he had been a good student who'd always submitted his work on time. And that frantic soul was absolutely of no help.

So I followed my worst instincts, told a friend on the team to inform the coach that I had to miss practice to finish a paper, and set about to explicate the subtleties of Beatrice. When I returned to practice after three days, the coach, without saying a word, simply consigned me to the bench. My theory that he would understand my value and eventually restore me to my starting role proved false. It soon became evident that he had no intention of putting me back where I had once been. Effectively, I was through. My culpability notwithstanding, I found this excessive. I had been punished, no doubt appropriately; why couldn't my sin be forgiven and I be allowed to start again? I was still the same player I had been before my fateful decision. The coach, however, certainly didn't see things this way: regardless of my ability, I had lost that privilege.

Several weeks into my benching, I told Coach Munro that if I wasn't going to play, there appeared to be no reason for me to stay on the team, secretly (or perhaps not so secretly) hoping he would seek to avoid such a traumatic loss by letting me back into his good graces. But he was either too shrewd for that or too insensitive. "What will you do for your athletic credits if you leave?" he responded, undercutting all my fantasies of his caring. "Think it over and let me know." I decided to stay. I played in dribs and drabs, but never again as the starting guard he had originally made me.

We had a relatively mediocre team and endured a dismal season, losing more games than we won. Our last opponent was undefeated Yale, featuring Johnny Lee, a high school all-American from Brooklyn who went on to become a college all-American and a draft choice of the New York Knicks. The game was never in doubt. The only issue: Would Yale break 100 points in crushing us? (They did.) At halftime Mr. Munro gave a kind of farewell speech, thanking us for our effort and saying how much he had enjoyed coaching us. As we couldn't possibly beat Yale, he felt he wanted to give those boys who had never played previously an opportunity to start in the second half. And in this group of earnest misfits, whom I silently characterized as the lame, the halt, and the blind, he included me, the person he had chosen as captain for the first game. How far the favored have fallen, I reflected. But then, as we walked out onto the court, he sidled up to me and whispered words that made me feel that perhaps at the end he had decided that I deserved better. I chose to receive them, in any case, as a kind of gesture of forgiveness. "You're captain this half," he instructed me. "You guard Lee."

Janitor

Harvard has always insisted that it trains leaders—in government, business, education, science—and that is no doubt true. Generally not included in the list of occupations for which the college allegedly prepares you is janitor, the first serious job I took in the fall of 1958, after graduation. Having flown to Madison to begin graduate school at the University of Wisconsin, I confronted the unavoidable shock of incipient adult life: the need to find a place to live. The Harvard housing office was no longer going to take care of me. Instead I got a map of the area around the school, a list of approved boardinghouses, and started my search. My requirements were simple. I wanted privacy. No shared bathroom, no shared kitchen, no roommate. Just my own space. Size didn't matter, as long as it was mine alone.

Not easy to find, I discovered, as I walked up countless staircases and looked into countless unsatisfactory arrangements. Finally I located a possibility that, if not distinguished, was at least minimally appropriate to meeting my criteria for privacy. Talking to my prospective landlady, I noticed that she seemed to be examining me rather searchingly. "Are you American?" she asked, after a few minutes of conversation.

"Sure," I replied jovially, thinking it odd but attributing it, perhaps, to some midwestern concerns that I didn't fully understand.

"Were you born here?" she continued, obviously troubled by something in my speech.

"Yes. Absolutely, right in New York."

"You have a funny accent," she said. "Are your parents American?"

Now the joviality began to drain from me as I stared at her. "Yes," I said stonily.

She continued: "Do you speak English at home?"

I assured her I did. Although I suppose that at this point I should have seen where she was heading, I was sufficiently perplexed by her grilling that I had no idea what was happening.

Her next question, however, solved the mystery of why my apparently peculiar way of speaking bothered her. "Are you Jewish?" she asked, having triumphantly concluded what was wrong with me.

I cannot remember how I responded—I assume I confessed—other than to say I wasn't interested in her room. My anger was vitiated by the insane humor of the situation. All those years at Harvard perfecting my WASP accent and manner, and this somewhat slovenly landlady immediately detected my speaking Jewish! How was that possible? What do Jews sound like, I wondered, as I left the building.

No one else discovered my Jewish identity as I continued to walk the streets of Madison. Finally, in a small private house on lovely Langdon Street, I found the tiny lodging of my dreams: a minuscule apartment, gerrymandered out of a space behind the owner's kitchen, in which the sofa bed, when extended, went from back wall to door, with its own bathroom and a functional if Lilliputian-sized kitchen. Perfect in every way, except for one minor problem: the occupant had to agree to serve as the entire building's janitor. For which the generous owner, retired dentist Dr. Peter Barsness, would reduce the rent by twenty dollars a month. So instead of sixty-five dollars, I could have my privacy for only forty-five, easily manageable on my graduate teaching assistant's stipend. And the duties would not be onerous, Dr. Barsness emphasized. Looking after things, putting the trash out, cleaning the several bathrooms and stairwells for the other tenants, and doing a little shoveling of snow during the winter. If the snow was heavy, Dr. B would get the city to keep the sidewalk and the path to the garage, at the back of the house, clear. In addition, in the fall, I would be responsible for keeping the rather large front porch free from the leaves that would flutter down from the trees overlooking the house.

It all seemed reasonable and affordable. If I didn't especially relish the thought of cleaning other people's toilets, as it was in the service of earning me my sought-after privacy, it was worth it. So in I squeezed with my meager belongings and vast trunkloads of anxiety about the start of my teaching career.

I was stiff, humorless, and infinitely boring in my freshman composition class, droning on about where to put commas and other assorted rules of grammar. I remained too nervous ever to smile, a point made by Mrs. Thomas, the director of the composition program, who observed one of my classes. She suggested that an encouraging smile every now and then might be a good idea. I knew she was right, but I was incapable of such a relaxed response. Sternness seemed the only way to beat down my panic.

Although sweeping leaves off the porch and the sidewalk in front of the house required no preparation, it normally took two to three hours to accomplish, hours I felt I could not spare, given my hysteria about getting ready for my two-days-a-week classes. I swept and swept, but the leaves never stopped falling, and Dr. B never stopped haranguing me about my janitorial failures. He viewed with contempt my extraordinary efforts to keep his porch leaf-free and his toilets sparkling. He rarely talked to me directly about his dissatisfaction, but he didn't have to. Instead, I would wake in the morning (remember, my apartment backed on his kitchen) to hear him reviling me over his coffee. "Mother," he would bark in his raspy voice (he had a charming way of referring to his wife as "Mother"), "he's no damn good." No matter how hard I tried, I was never any damn good. Mother, who couldn't stand up to the abrasive Dr. B, would occasionally invoke the "he seems like such a nice young man to me" line, but to no avail. He would have none of it. A bad teacher by my own standards, I was even a worse janitor by Dr. B's.

It was not a fun fall. I was in a constant state of tension over my teaching, resenting the hours I had to commit to the care of 135 Langdon Street. I recall one moment with great clarity. I had just finished vacuuming the stairway's runner from basement to attic and was now on my knees, attended by a bucket of soapy water, as per my instructions, scrubbing the sides of the stairs. Suddenly I noticed several perfectly formed, brown, marble-shaped objects lying next to the carpet. I couldn't quite make out what they were, so I picked them up and sniffed. At that point they unmistakably declared themselves to be dog shit. "What is wrong with this picture?" I thought. "Here I am, a Harvard graduate, allegedly destined for some kind of distinguished career, on my knees, cleaning stairs, several pieces of dog poop in my hand, which I am holding up to my nose, the better to identify them. Is there any hope?" I didn't think so.

The hours spent sweeping in the fall were nothing compared to those shoveling in the winter. Dr. B's claim that he would get help from the city if the snow was heavy seemed to have been conveniently forgotten when the snows actually began. The winter of '59 was acknowledged to be the worst in years. It would take me two or three hours to clear the street and porch and walkways, after which I would hear over the radio that another foot and a half was expected in short order. It never stopped and I never stopped. The morning complaints to Mother became more vitriolic. At the beginning of the winter, Dr. B would come up the outside staircase to my apartment to rap on the door and yell at me. I was proud of myself for fashioning a brilliant solution to end this kind of torment. I stopped shoveling the snow off the stairway, permitting it to ice over into a kind of mini-Alpine challenge. While I could hoist myself up by clinging to the banister, Dr. B., neither the youngest (he was eighty-five) nor the spryest, would not even attempt to ascend the ice mountain I had produced, leaving me blessedly free from his verbal assaults. I should add that during one of my endless shoveling sessions I met the janitor of the building next door, and learned that not only were his duties fewer than mine, with his landlord-owner frequently not in residence, but he paid no rent at all. Such is the price of privacy, however, I told myself as I soldiered on, scrubbing, shoveling, being vilified to Mother over morning coffee.

Having swept Dr. B through the fall and shoveled him through the winter, I looked forward to the spring—when, as far as I could see, nothing would fall from the heavens that would despoil his porch and sidewalk (at least nothing that I would be required to remove), and I would finally be able to focus on my teaching and my own academic work, like every other normal graduate student. Unfortunately, he was one step ahead of me. He said he had to have a full-time janitor who was always available, not one flirting with life outside of 135 Langdon Street. He had unearthed a retired couple, obviously down on their luck, happy to be jammed into the same restricted space I had barely been able to navigate by myself. My janitorial services, in short, were no longer wanted.

JANITOR

Dr. B informed me that the replacement couple was coming the following week. We thanked each other for the opportunity—I didn't let on that I had not appreciated hearing myself excoriated in the early morning week after week—and off I went in search of another place. By this time, privacy had ceased to matter and I was content to share a bathroom in your standard student boardinghouse. I spent the spring and summer semesters completing my MA, after which I decamped for Columbia. Living with my parents for the first time in five years had its agonies, but they did not include trying to sort out dog turds from other types of spherical objects.

Garbage, Faculty

"Garbage, faculty!"

This cry, repeated several times a day, emanated from the second-floor window of the southwestern side of Low Memorial Library, otherwise known as President Grayson Kirk's office, currently being occupied—it was late April 1968—by angry Columbia students. Eager to humiliate the faculty who were standing guard on the ledge surrounding the library, protecting their right to protest, the students summoned them to receive the large plastic bags of garbage generated by life in the presidential suite. Answering the call, one of the younger teachers—preceptors, instructors, assistant professors—would clamber up the metal grille on one of the first-floor windows, extend one arm upward while clinging to the bars with the other, and dutifully accept the garbage offering. The students were delighted. The faculty, earnest in defense of their students, seemed happy to be playing a role. The garbage, after all, had to be removed.

Our presence on the ledge (I was an instructor in the English department, lithe enough to climb up the window's grille but unwilling to do so) had come about through endless deliberations conducted by the faculty, attempting to find a negotiated peace to the crisis.

The lounge in Philosophy Hall had turned into the site of all-day discussions about the occupation and what to do about it. That the students had little interest in our philosophical anguish did not seem to occur to anybody immersed in the lounge debates. But if talk failed to provide a solution, the least we could do was provide our bodies to demonstrate our allegiance to those undergraduates in Kirk's office, keep them from harm, and generally bear witness to what was going on. The administration couldn't pull a fast one—like trying to slip in the police to clear out the office—if we were on guard. To this end it was agreed that faculty members, identified by white handkerchiefs tied around our arms, would occupy the ledge.

Once on the ledge, things got complicated, as rules of engagement had to be established so that faculty members would understand their duties. Not a problem for professors, of course; the day after we took to the ledge, a flyer was distributed, authorship unknown, outlining our responsibilities.

The most important clause had to do with turf ownership: it was made absolutely clear that only authorized faculty could inhabit the ledge. This meant that no students, either those sympathetic to the occupiers or those against, could set foot there.

More elaborate were rules relating to the conveying of food to the protesters. Because no one was permitted to enter or leave Low, the sole means of providing them with nourishment required hurling loaves of bread, cold cuts, processed cheese, and the like from outside Low to the grateful recipients waiting in the second-floor windows for their gift packages. This was made more difficult than it might otherwise have been when a group of undergraduates, largely athletes, opposed to the strike and eager to get in on some kind of action, formed themselves into the so-called Majority Coalition, by all odds the smallest organization of students. In addition to marching around the campus, protesting the protesters, they established as their territory the ground between the faculty-patrolled ledge and a hedge, fifteen feet or so to the west of the library, facing the ledge. Their mission was twofold: to ensure that no supporter try to get into the building and to force those attempting to supply those within to fling their packages from outside the hedge, maximizing the possibility of errant throws.

Our published instructions tried to account for all exigencies. The most important stipulation had to do with food that missed its target and fell to the ledge. To protect our professorial neutrality, under no circumstances were we permitted to throw it back up to the window. At that point the supplies belonged to us, not the students, and could not be given to them. The rule was absolute. Any violation of this restriction would be punishable by expulsion from the ledge. Food that bounced off the library but did not land on the ledge, however, was not ours but the Majority Coalition's, and we were not expected to contest ownership. We were charged with making sure that neither Majority Coalitionists nor colleagues of the strikers gained access to the ledge. Garbage removal remained a voluntary activity, not covered in our guidelines.

Although I found our position as guardians of the ledge to be fairly absurd, two moments stood out for me. The first occurred when a professor of philosophy, perhaps more sympathetic to those inside Kirk's office than his fellows, did the unthinkable. When an errant loaf of bread found its way to the ledge and landed at his feet, he bent down and, with due deliberateness, picked it up and threw it to the waiting students in the window. We were all dumbfounded. A chorus of cheers burst out from beyond the hedge, in praise of his courageous behavior. Cries of execration were showered upon him from the outraged Majority Coalition. The response was swift.

GARBAGE, FACULTY

He was escorted from the ledge in disgrace, amid healthy booing. I wondered whether he would be permitted to return the next day, but he never came back. I suspect he would not have been allowed to, even if he had appealed for redemption.

The second incident involved a breaching of the faculty's control of the ledge by the Majority Coalition. Although I was standing right there, I was unaware of why it happened. All I know is that without warning or any clear motivation, several students popped onto the ledge. Perhaps they were testing our resolve or were simply eager for some physical confrontation, as hanging around between hedge and ledge, insulting the strike's supporters, was not an entirely fulfilling activity. Whatever the reason for the encroachment, we responded magnificently. We promptly surrounded the trespassers and wrestled them off the ledge.

Although this event was surprising, nothing was particularly astonishing about it. The astonishing part followed. Apparently in the brief tussle, one of the intruders got scratched and began bleeding slightly. As we reestablished our decorum on the ledge, we found ourselves being excoriated by the coalition's leader, a college senior. I remember his words exactly: "One of my men is bleeding, a man who had never done anything wrong in his life is bleeding, and it's your fault!" I was mesmerized by the claims of purity regarding the injured student, his instant rhetorical transformation from student to man, the moral badgering we, the august faculty, were receiving at the hands of someone who several days before we were teaching in our classrooms.

The lunacy of life on the ledge—fetching bags of garbage, dismissing faculty in shame for improper behavior, fighting off interlopers, being upbraided by self-appointed student leaders—served as a neat microcosm of the madness that engulfed the campus that week in April.

SCRAPS, ORTS, AND FRAGMENTS

Perhaps the best analysis of what was going on at Columbia is not to be found in *The Strawberry Statement* or *Up Against the Ivy Wall* but, rather, in a book written several thousand years earlier, Thucydides's *History of the Peloponnesian War*. His brilliant examination of how the revolution in Corcyra changed language itself speaks also to the dynamics of the Columbia revolution:

> To fit in with the change of events, words, too, had to change their usual meanings. What used to be described as a thoughtless act of aggression was now regarded as the courage one would expect to find in a party member; to think of the future and wait was merely another way of saying one was a coward; any idea of moderation was just an attempt to disguise one's unmanly character; ability to understand a question from all sides meant that one was totally unfitted for action.

The word that disappeared entirely during the student uprising was "student." In the new world that no longer was willing to accept traditional power roles, there were no students. There were protesters, strikers, steering committee members, negotiators, runners (to carry messages between buildings), and Majority Coalition members. And lest anyone think that classroom buildings were being illegally occupied, they became communes, and those staying within them, communards.

In pointing out the absurdity of much that was going on around us, I don't mean to trivialize the events of '68. There was genuine anger, there were real issues (some), and there were committed students (some). But the experience has become so clotted in solemnity that it is useful to remember that while serious things were happening, some students also were having a very good time: the subjects of intense media attention, self-important in their deliberations, excited by their power in closing down the university. A candlelit procession around the campus celebrated a New Age marriage. Postrevolutionary curricular guidelines were formulated to replace traditional, no longer relevant, ones. Now anybody could teach anything. Courses would no longer be the prerogative of stuffy types with PhDs.

The flight to fantasy was not just appealing to students. But the fantasies pursued by the faculty had to do not with remaking the university in a more democratic model but in asserting the power of rational discourse to solve problems. The faculty counted on its stock-in-trade—talk, subtle, compelling, earnest—to bridge the gulf between administration and students. That neither faction cared what solutions the faculty were capable of devising didn't affect the torrent of talk that filled 301 Philosophy Hall from morning to night. You could stop by anytime you wanted to hear why amnesty was wrong, why it was right, why black students had to be treated differently from white, why the police should be permitted to clear the buildings, or why they shouldn't be allowed on the campus.

The Philosophy Hall lounge also served as the place where the administration would communicate its thinking to the faculty. A senior dean, elevated to emissary-in-chief, would periodically appear before the assembled faculty to explain what the president and vice president wanted us to know. It was not a pleasant job. The facts he shared remained scanty, and the faculty, disgruntled at being kept out of the highest level of deliberations, did not receive his briefings cordially. I witnessed one of the more terrible moments of this interaction. The dean was being harshly questioned by faculty who were outraged by his uninformative report. He was clearly exhausted; he might well have been drunk. Suddenly he snarled at one relentless professor, "All right, I'll tell you what's happening," and then began mumbling, making very little sense. The embarrassment was palpable; the solution unclear. I was sitting next to two departmental administrative assistants, who were horrified: "We've got to get him out of here." They conspired together, and then one of them went outside the lounge. A few seconds later she reentered, walked up to the dean, who was struggling unsuccessfully to be coherent, and whispered in his ear. "I'm sorry, I have to stop. The president needs to see me," he announced to us, and left.

I spent the days leading up to the coming bust doing my duty on the ledge and trying to fathom what might be happening by listening intently to the interminable talk in the lounge. As no one had access to any real information, our questions couldn't be answered. We had no idea how or when the occupation would end.

In retrospect, given the unreality of everything that was going on, it made perfect sense that I would learn, in the early hours of April 30 from the bartender at the West End Bar, on Broadway near 114th Street, that the police were coming to clear the buildings. If the president wouldn't tell us, at least we could count on the bartenders. I finished my beer and immediately returned to the campus. Looking for a strategic place to plant myself, I headed for the south door of Fayerweather, where faculty members were gathering. Passing in front of the security entrance of Low Library, I beheld a chilling, somewhat surreal sight: large numbers of thick-necked men, clearly not students, came flowing out of the building, all disguised in sweatshirts from different colleges—Adelphi, City College, NYU. The better to pretend they were not policemen but innocent college students? Colored buttons worn near the neck ensured that when they set about beating up students who got close to them, they wouldn't be fighting with each other. I have never understood to this day whom they thought they were fooling.

As the uniformed police faced us in front of Fayerweather, I spotted F. W. Dupee, a marvelous professor of English whom I revered. I resolved that whatever happened I would stick with him and try to prevent him from getting hurt. He alarmed me when he admitted that he regretted wearing his expensive new dentures before the upcoming police action, but I felt this was no time to confess fear. Not to an older man I admired. The police, clenching small blackjacks, urged those of us in front of the building, now some twenty or twenty-five strong, to disband, but we could hardly just go away. Instead we burst into "We Shall Overcome" and waited for the police to come at us, which they promptly did. Having exhibited our courage, we were then free to scatter. I pushed Fred ahead of me toward the St. Paul campus exit, receiving a few indifferent punches on my back and shoulders in the process. But Fred, eager not to miss the assault, looked back over my shoulder, earning a majestic black eye for his troubles. The next day Jimmy Wechsler, the feisty editor of the *New York Post* and a Columbia alumnus, condemned the police for "working over" Fred Dupee. Fred received congratulations for his heroism and toughness; only the two of us knew that he had not been singled out by vengeful cops but hit by a wild punch that he never should have turned around to receive in the first place.

The police were efficient in emptying the buildings. They were also violent—unnecessarily so. After a week of being insulted by students, who delighted in calling them "pigs," it would be unreasonable to assume they would opt for gentle behavior. They didn't appreciate being treated with contempt by those they considered spoiled kids, who were trashing an institution they would have loved their own children to be able to attend. Clearing the campus was payback time, and the police made sure to deliver their message unambiguously. If not defensible, it was at least understandable.

The consequences of the "revolution" were all too real for the institution: seven hundred students arrested, the president and vice president losing their jobs, and alumni financial support severely damaged. It would take years, a new administration, new governing structures, like a university senate, and overhauled disciplinary procedures for it to recover. I personally was stunned by the mass craziness that had swept over Columbia, by the ease with which people fled from reality in illustrating Thucydides's insights into the frailties of human nature. If one wanted the perfect conclusion to the week's madness, it was provided not by the students or faculty or administrators or police but by Dr. Frode Jensen, a Columbia trustee who was not on campus for the bust and therefore knew nothing about what went on. He was asked by the *Columbia Daily Spectator* the next day about the allegations of police brutality, a subject not dear to the heart of any trustee. In one superb, solipsistic pronouncement he took refuge in his own alternative reality, in which it was easier to live: "There was no police brutality," he insisted. "It didn't occur."

Academic Assassination

The invitation was pleasantly straightforward: Would I like to join a small number of faculty members and graduate students to see a brief film made by Quentin Bell, Virginia Woolf's art-historian nephew, of Monk's House, the Woolfs' country cottage in Rodmell? As a young assistant professor in the English department at Columbia teaching a course on the Bloomsbury writers and working on a book on Virginia Woolf, I could hardly object. And yet I knew with absolute certainty that attending this event would doom my chances for tenure in the department. There was no logical way to justify this feeling—and there certainly was no way to refuse to go—but as I smiled my happy assent I realized that I was smiling at my impending academic demise. I didn't know how, and I didn't know why, but there was not the faintest doubt in my mind that this was the end. The memorable words of a pornographic movie I had recently seen with my friends George and Peter flashed across my mind. "Welcome to my humiliation," the jolly host announced to all those who came to witness and participate in his forthcoming degradation. Although the viewers wouldn't be coming to see me, I felt an instant rapport with him.

SCRAPS, ORTS, AND FRAGMENTS

It was the spring of 1973, and both the invitation and the source of my foreboding came from Carolyn Heilbrun, the senior professor of contemporary British literature at Columbia. Revered now as the godmother or grandmother of the academic feminist movement, Carolyn had struggled through to her full professorship in the face of what she considered at the very least the disregard, or at worst the overt hostility, of the overwhelmingly male English department. She felt undervalued and underpaid, initially consigned by the old boys' club to teach in the School of General Studies, the adult branch of the university, instead of the more prestigious Columbia College, presided over by the elegance and eminence of Lionel Trilling, whom she clearly detested. (In one of the mysteries she wrote under the pen name of Amanda Cross, she contrived to have Quentin Anderson, a colleague of Trilling's, murder him in the elevator of a Columbia classroom building.) Unquestionably Carolyn had come of scholarly age during the awful prehistoric era for female academics, when opportunities were limited and male dismissiveness more or less the norm. By the time I became an assistant professor in 1970, she was nurturing a full range of personal and professional grievances, angry at her own situation and at the larger predicament of aspiring women professors.

Without understanding it, I had exacerbated her sense of professional injustice by having proposed my course on the Bloomsbury group of writers and artists, including Virginia Woolf. I had not appreciated, nor had anyone warned me, that Carolyn thought of them as comprising her turf. Inasmuch as Columbia had never offered such a course (which Carolyn could have done whenever she wanted to), I saw no reason to think I was trespassing on private grounds when I suggested mine. Worse, I later learned, I didn't see any reason, having invented it, that I should consult with her about its formulation. I naïvely thought myself perfectly capable of putting together an interesting syllabus on my own. In retrospect, of course, my political errors were staggering, but it simply never occurred to me that my "Bloomsbury circle" course could be construed as part of the department's agenda to demean Professor Heilbrun. I should have known better.

But I certainly knew enough to understand that she was not one of my great admirers, which contributed to the gnawing certainty that, in some way impossible to anticipate, I would not emerge unscathed from the film. Finally the day of the screening arrived. It was to be shown in the penthouse apartment of the woman who owned Charivari, a series of stylish clothing shops around the city, whose daughter was a graduate student working with Carolyn. As I approached the apartment I imagined the scene I thought would follow. There would be polite blather while the twenty or so of us assembled, munched on some light appetizers, drank some too-sweet white wine, and then sat down to watch the film. When it was finished, we would get up from our chairs and engage in a more sustained social interaction, nibbling on the odd nut or two and imbibing some more wine or perhaps a gin and tonic, as we chatted amiably about Bloomsbury in particular and life in general. In other words, in my vision, the film would be the occasion of a pleasant if low-end cocktail party.

The chairs in the large living room were arranged in horseshoe fashion, with a screen at the open end, a projector at the other. There was no drink in sight, although once we were seated a small bowl of nuts managed to make its way punctiliously around the horseshoe. The atmosphere was decidedly more sacred than secular: conversation was constrained and slightly awkward, as if we were attending a solemn religious service rather than simply seeing a documentary movie. After a few introductory words of thanks by Carolyn for the use of the apartment, the film began.

SCRAPS, ORTS, AND FRAGMENTS

Bell devoted its thirty-three minutes to taking us on an intimate guided tour of the interior of Monk's House, lovingly discussing all the furnishings—tables and chairs, ceramics, rugs, curtains, kitchenware, and the like—which had either been manufactured in or at least inspired by Roger Fry's Omega Workshops. Fry, a close friend of the Woolfs' and arguably England's most influential modernist art critic during the early decades of the twentieth century, had sought to infuse Post-impressionist vitality and color into the relatively somber world of British decorative arts. In the service of this idea, he had started the Omega Workshops in London in 1913, to encourage young artists to experiment with new conceptions of interior design. However admirable the theory, much of the practice, to my jaundiced eye, was quite awful, particularly their commitment to adorning perfectly nice furniture with bright, garish colors. Fascinating as it was to see Bell make his informed way through the Omega Workshops–influenced paintings, furniture, and fabrics the Woolfs had collected, I remained unimpressed.

And that was the problem. Or at least part of it. As the projector flicked off and the lights went on, I sat in quiet expectation that the next phase of the evening, as I had conceived it, would begin. No one stirred, however, and I rapidly concluded that the notion that there would be a next phase of the evening existed only in my imagination. Instead, with all of us stiffly rooted in our chairs, people began to make sensitive comments about the glories of Bloomsbury culture, the beauty of Monk's House, the extraordinary achievement of the Omega Workshops. I have always found situations of mandatory reverence to be extremely unnerving, tending to cause all my cerebral functions to shut down. With graduate students vying with one another to score critical points with Carolyn, I knew I had to say something to attest to my Bloomsbury seriousness, but I could think of no appropriate expostulation of delight. I was in a state of total paralysis. And then suddenly the hideous demon of self-destructiveness took possession of me, and before I could suppress it I heard myself blurt out that what I found interesting was the fact that despite the exquisite aesthetic sensitivity of the Woolfs and their circle, so much of the furniture and ceramics was actually pretty dreadful.

I could almost feel the air being sucked out of the room as the others struggled to digest what had just been uttered. No one responded. The spiritual vulgarity I had just revealed had transported me well beyond the bounds of civilized discourse where one might legitimately expect an answer. It was as if I had not spoken at all. I knew immediately that I had committed an egregiousness, but I had no sense of how to rectify it. Desultory comments continued as I desperately pondered ways to make things better. By this time, of course, too frazzled to think clearly, I occupied the unenviable position (although I wasn't aware of it then) of more or less guaranteeing that whatever I came up with would probably make things worse. And worse they became. When someone volunteered that you could actually rent Monk's House for the summer through Britain's National Landmarks Trust, I responded, in an effort to add a bit of harmless levity, that I had recently noticed in the *New York Review of Books* that Marianne Moore's Washington Square apartment was also available for summer rental. (While I fully accept my culpability in daring to criticize the Woolfs' artistic taste, I still maintain that the Moore quip did not deserve the implicit rebuke it earned. I wasn't, after all, suggesting that Moore was a greater writer than Woolf.) The result was the same, however: more silent obloquy heaped upon me.

Immersed in my terminal shame, I still clung to the hope that if we could be released from our seats I might be able to redeem myself through the healing agency of casual social conversation. But following a fusillade of more adoring Bloomsbury appreciation, that possibility was quashed by Carolyn summarily declaring, "Let's see it again." Having just seen all thirty-three minutes of it, and having a very clear memory of the various artifacts I disliked, I did not understand why I had to see it again. Using the (lame) excuse of the need to relieve my six-month-old son's babysitter, I completed my trifecta of unconscionables by explaining to Carolyn that I had to go. I thanked her profusely, but I could tell she wasn't fooled in the least. "I think you are not entirely sympathetic to the Bloomsbury sensibility," she sweetly intoned, certifying that I had in fact managed to bring about everything I'd feared: I was a goner. If I had any doubts about this, they were resolved several weeks later. Speaking to a junior colleague who approved of me, I learned that he had been told by a colleague who didn't approve (and who had been at the screening) that I had acted "very badly" during that evening.

The only question that remained was precisely how my academic death sentence would be administered. Several months later, I found out. At the time, the procedure for a tenure vote in the English department required a group of three senior faculty members to evaluate each junior professor being considered and to make a recommendation to the department as a whole regarding the candidate's qualifications. My subcommittee—including Carolyn—submitted a strongly positive assessment, calling for me to be proposed for promotion.

But then Carolyn asked to speak, saying that although she had signed the report, she had to express certain reservations about me. She proceeded to explain in great and totally fictitious detail how uncooperative a member of the department I had been, how I refused to serve on committees, read her students' work, sit on exams, help with doctoral orals, advise on dissertations, or engage in practically any of the activities normally expected of a junior faculty member. All of this, of course, was a complete fabrication. I was one of those—I believe the technical term is "schlemiels"—who always did everything he was asked, never once turning down a professorial request for my participation.

Faculty being faculty (which is to say, not people eager for confrontation), no one bothered to question Carolyn's scathing denunciation of my uncollegiality, though everyone who really knew me knew the accusations couldn't possibly be true. After she was through lying about me, there was no case left for nominating me for tenure. What department, after all, would want to live for the next thirty years with someone so pathologically unpleasant and unhelpful? But as it was known that I was currently being considered for the job of the college's associate dean, it was resolved simply to moot the whole affair rather than bring it to its by now unavoidably negative conclusion. And so it was that in the spring I became a dean without any official departmental action being taken on my tenure.

Although a full-time administrator when the fall term began, I was still a member of the English department, and continued to do (Carolyn's testimony notwithstanding) anything it asked me to do, such as sit on doctoral orals. I also continued to work on my Woolf manuscript and to accept any assignments I got for book reviews. Sometime in October the *New York Times Book Review*, for which I had previously written, asked me for a substantial piece on Quentin Bell's biography of his aunt Virginia. It was published early in November as a front-page review. Immediately after it came out, I was told by two different students in Carolyn's doctoral seminar that she walked into class and without any provocation or introduction began to criticize it, arguing not only that it was unsatisfactory, but that I didn't like Woolf and had simply "latched onto her because she was a good thing." I was, needless to say, incensed at the spurious allegations regarding my attitude toward Woolf, not to speak of the blatant unprofessionalism of discussing a faculty colleague (however disliked) in front of a group of students. I could hardly argue that Carolyn was obliged to like my work, but it did seem unacceptable that she was entitled to spread lies about my character and behavior around the university with total impunity. As faculty wouldn't and students couldn't, I realized that I had to try to deal with this myself.

Several weeks after she had reviled me in her seminar, an opportunity presented itself. Ironically, it was at one of those doctoral orals on which she claimed I never sat. Following the two-hour exam, at which I was one of two questioners in the candidate's major field—Carolyn was the other—I asked if I could speak with her for a minute. I told her that I had heard what she had said about me in her seminar, and that while I recognized her right to be displeased with my work, she certainly had no right to lie about me and my reasons for writing on Woolf. She smiled, said how pleased she was that I had spoken to her, and agreed to come to my office after lunch (it was now noon) to clarify matters.

She arrived at two o'clock, unquestionably not quite as happy to be there as her earlier smile had suggested. She began by admitting that she had said things about me—but then added that she was aware that I had said things about her. I pointed out that I had heard from a number of people about her diatribe at my tenure meeting, and suggested that levying charges against me that she knew were utterly false was not inclined to make me one of her avid supporters. How could she have acted that way?

Her response startled me. "What could I do?" she answered plaintively. "There I was, surrounded by Stade, Said, and Marcus. What could I do?"

ACADEMIC ASSASSINATION

I confess I was taken aback by the shocking inversion taking place, in which I was being asked to sympathize with her. The assistant professor who was defamed should understand the predicament of the full professor who had defamed him. Hemmed in by three male-chauvinist professors, the weird logic followed, what could she do but lie about me? I gawked silently at her, finding it difficult to process what I was hearing. She went on, building the case that instead of the innocent object of her vituperation I imagined myself to be, I was actually connected to the malign male conspiracy that had oppressed her throughout her career. "You young men are so skilled at dealing with women as secretaries, mistresses, and wives," she said, chastising me, "but you have no idea how to relate to women as professional equals." In the class-action suit she was bringing against the powerful old boys' academic network, the mere fact that I was most certainly not a member provided no refuge: my assistant professorial insignificance notwithstanding, I was as guilty as all the rest.

Having explained to her satisfaction why she felt justified in libeling me, she next turned to my Bell review, assuring me that not only did she not like it, none of her friends did, either. (All of my friends, on the other hand—and all of my family—did, but I saw no reason to make this case.) In emphasizing its inadequacy, she added the extraordinary comment that "it would have been crazy of you to pass it up," making it clear that we all knew that she should have been asked to do it, not me. Since, in fact, I thought I was a perfectly appropriate reviewer, I was stunned by the implication that I must have recognized that Carolyn was the proper choice. The deliberate snubbing of the qualified Carolyn for the unqualified Rosenthal made eminent sense to her because it was another aspect of the plot against her. This time it was not old Columbia professors but the young, male *Book Review* editors, people like John Leonard and Richard Locke, who were working to deprive her of her rightful place in the scholarly sun. Miraculously enough, in the same way that I was in part responsible for the department's dismissive treatment of Carolyn, I was also apparently in league with scheming editors at the paper. If only, I thought, as the charges piled up against me, I actually possessed some small portion of the evil influence I was said to be endlessly exercising.

Beyond trying to point out that as somebody acutely sensitive to power relations in institutions, she had to acknowledge that she had used her tenured seniority to lash out at somebody who was in no position to respond, I did little to defend myself. I didn't argue over the quality of my prose, my credentials for writing on Bloomsbury, or the purity of my character. I mostly listened as she documented my intellectual and moral failings. After about an hour or so, we agreed that it had been a valuable conversation and said we hoped it might be the beginning of a more cordial relationship. We shook hands and she promised that she would no longer say anything negative about me. And as far as I know, she never did.

Associate Dean

It would not be metaphoric in the least to assert that my career as a dean began with a bang—or, more accurately, six bangs, although only five actually counted. It was late July 1972 and the new dean of Columbia College, a young British classicist with the silly name of Peter Pouncey, had just elevated me from the position of assistant professor in the English department to his associate dean. He then went off to Wales for his summer vacation. I had been on the job for two weeks, without the slightest idea of what deans did in general or I was supposed to do in particular. Without Peter there to instruct me, I saw no reason to hang around the hot city. So I borrowed a friend's car and, with my almost-eight-months-pregnant wife and two stepsons, went off to a lakeside cottage in Maine. Because no one had ever cared about my summer plans during my previous incarnation as a member of the English department, it never occurred to me that with the dean away it might be prudent to let someone in my office know how to contact the newly hatched associate dean, should the need arise. Besides, nothing ever happened in the summer anyway. Mumbling something about Maine, I packed up and headed northward, leaving no address, phone number, or even vague approximation about where in Maine I might be found.

Several days after we arrived, Judith and I were sitting on a tattered sofa practicing, as we obsessively did, our breathing exercises in preparation for a September natural birth. Timing her while we worked together on the proper rhythm of shallow breathing, I was startled to hear the heavy thumping of boots on the stairs leading to our cottage, followed by a decisive knocking on our door. I opened it to find myself staring at the stomach of what seemed to be the largest state trooper in the world, fully attired in black leather everythings and sporting the appropriately ominous mirrored sunglasses.

"Michael Rosenthal?" he inquired. "Yes, sir," I replied, employing my best deferential manner in the face of gigantic state troopers. "Call your office," he ordered. "Something's happened and they want to speak to you." I thanked him and he clumped away, leaving me bewildered both by the fact that I might be needed, although I couldn't imagine what service I could possibly provide so early in my deanhood, and by the fact that I had been discovered despite having left no forwarding address of any kind.

Obviously a phone call would solve these mysteries, but first I had to locate a phone, as we didn't have one. A kindly neighbor gave me access to hers, and I soon learned that something had indeed happened. Harry Coleman, the dean of students, whose office was down the hall from mine in Hamilton Hall, had just placed a failing student on academic suspension for a year. Unhappy with the decision, the student apparently thought it was appropriate to express his dissatisfaction by getting a .38 revolver from his dormitory room, going to the dean's office, and blasting away at point-blank range. Five bullets hit Coleman; the sixth left a trail across the top of a New York phone book and lodged in a wall. The student then ran off, never to be found. (Miraculously, Coleman survived, continuing as dean for another five years before retiring.)

ASSOCIATE DEAN

I listened with horror to the report from my assistant, culminating in the insistence that as I was the college's senior administrator (by default), it was essential that I return immediately to the dean's office to take charge. I naturally agreed, though I had to admit that calming anxieties about the shooting of deans when I had been one for only two weeks had nothing to do with the challenges of the job as Peter had explained them to me. But back I went the next day, trying to convince myself that there was no one better qualified to do this, even if I had no idea how to proceed.

Once in the office I decided that projecting cheery confidence was the correct approach, so reaching into the bag of administrative clichés, I summoned everybody together, explained what had happened, assured them that everything was under control, that Dean Coleman would recover, and that the school year would start as scheduled. I gave myself a reasonably high grade for this, my initial deanly performance, and began to think that perhaps I could do this job after all.

My first business phone call later that afternoon shattered my fragile optimism. The president of the alumni association informed me that he had prepared a statement to run in the next issue of the alumni magazine concerning the shooting. I had already understood that the college would have to have an official comment on the incident, and that it would be my responsibility to produce one for the magazine. A large and thorny dispute now arose. Whose magazine was it: the alumni association's, in which case the president of the association should presumably have the right to pronounce upon the event, or the college's, in which case the college administration (read: me) should respond? This rapidly developed ("degenerated" would be a better word) into a contentious argument, the lawyer-president, skilled in the litigious arts, battling the neophyte administrator. We published the magazine, I asserted, so it was ours; the alumni paid dues for it, he countered, so it belonged to them. Back and forth we went as I struggled to pretend that I thoroughly understood the somewhat vexed history of the college, the magazine, and the alumni association.

My attempt to project mastery of the facts was not made easier by the behavior of the assistant I had inherited from Peter. Uncertain—with good cause—about my capacity to conduct a proper defense of the college's position, she alternately rolled her eyes, twisted her mouth, and made unintelligible gestures with her hands as she monitored my end of the phone conversation. Her scrutiny made me feel like a competitive diver, anxiously looking about to see what score his efforts earned from the judges. But in place of a clearly printed number on a large electronic scoreboard, I encountered only the disturbing facial and digital gyrations generated by each of my complicated verbal maneuvers. Being observed by Doris was every bit as harrowing as trying to fend off the verbal assaults of my alumni antagonist. I had no choice, of course, but to blunder ahead, maintaining the authority of the college to write what it wanted, even as some of my more sophisticated rebuttals continued to elicit grimaces of disapproval from my skeptical assistant. Finally, after roughly an hour of unpleasant back-and-forth, lawyer Futter concluded that he had better—no doubt more profitable—things to do and mercifully terminated our conversation.

Although I knew that Doris had not necessarily been impressed, at least in my own eyes I had muddled through my first real trial as dean. I then composed a soothingly bland statement for the magazine, checked it with Peter by phone, and went home, comforting myself with the assessment that on balance I had measured up. (I had also learned how the giant state trooper had found me. Knowing that I was somewhere in Maine, my office had called the Maine State Police headquarters, informing them that I had to be located. In what I thought was a brilliant piece of sleuthing, the troopers contacted every summer rental agent in Maine until the name Rosenthal showed up on somebody's records. No fools, those state troopers.)

Relief over my survival did not last long. The next day, back in the office, I read in the *Times* that a spokesman for the university, commenting on the incident, had noted that "the university had a problem." I was aware that the university had many problems, but it was clear to me that the shooting of deans could not reasonably be included among them. I did not think it helpful to describe an obviously aberrant act in language that treated it as a common condition that invariably plagued us and that we needed to solve. Parents of prospective students, I felt confident, would not be pleased to think that our deans were being gunned down in their offices on a regular basis.

Seeing myself now as an administrator professionally responsible for the health of the institution, I thought I should convey my concern about how this was being handled to the university's president, William J. McGill. I had met McGill about a month before, when Peter, with me in tow, had paid him a courtesy call to introduce him to the college's new associate dean. A tough-talking, crew-cut type who had battled his way out of the Bronx, McGill did not appear to be overly enthusiastic about what he saw. When we left his office after a half hour's desultory conversation, I asked Peter why McGill had responded with such visceral loathing to me. Peter insisted I was imagining things and that it had all gone well. I remained unconvinced. But with the newly discovered protective instinct spawned in me by my administrative rank, I was not prepared to let spasms of self-doubt interfere with my desire to help the university through this crisis. So I called him.

"Bill," I began, addressing him in a familiar tone that drew upon our long friendship, "I think it's a mistake for us to refer to the shooting as a problem. Makes it seem as if deans are being shot all the time." I then learned my first lesson as a dean: Don't call the president with criticism of how his institution is managing a difficult situation, because he will surely decide you are attacking him.

McGill immediately lashed out at me, savaging my impudence, my ignorance, my indifference to the university's well-being. Having imagined that McGill would welcome my constructive insight, I found myself showered instead with presidential venom. After making it clear that I had no reason to bother him and nothing to offer, he then calmed down enough for me to respond feebly that I was merely trying to point out some of the semantic problems with the word "problem." He agreed and thanked me for my interest. I later came to understand that McGill—a former chair of Columbia's psychology department—believed strongly in the tactical use of the towering rage, fabricated to get him out of tight spots and undermine the opposition. Whether this was one of those conjured up for the occasion or a genuine emotional outburst I could never decide. Either way, it achieved its purpose and I never again presumed to share my wisdom with him.

In the space of two days, having assuaged the anxieties of a traumatized office, argued with the president of the alumni association, and alienated the president of the university, I felt ready to take on the demands of my new existence as associate dean, whatever they might be.

But what was I doing in such a position in the first place? How had I migrated from writing a book on Virginia Woolf as an assistant professor in the English department to being yelled at by the president of the university for trying to save the university from a self-inflicted public relations wound? People generally don't go to graduate school to get doctorates in literature in the hope of becoming deans. I had signed up to be a professor, not an administrator. I had never even bumped into a dean in my four years as a college student, and that seemed about right. Unlike Saul Bellow's dean, Albert Corde in *The Dean's December*, who "led the life of an executive in America," I entertained no executive aspirations.

Two years earlier I had taken on some administrative responsibility by consenting to direct the college's composition program, in response to a request that had originated with the English department, not me. (In the frantic quest for tenure in which all junior professors were engaged, one always did whatever the department wanted.) The appointment of Associate Dean Pouncey to Dean Pouncey meant, I was aware, that his earlier job had now become vacant, but it never occurred to me to consider it. To pursue deaning after only two years as a professor would constitute, I thought, serious personal failure.

Nevertheless, when a friend of mine, an assistant dean in the Dean of Students Office, suggested that perhaps I should be interested, I agreed to talk to Pouncey about it. My reasons were unabashedly base. The first, needless to say, had to do with money. As a third-year assistant professor in charge of the composition program, I was making $11,000. Although I had no idea what a deanly salary might be, I knew it had to be more than that. And having recently married a woman with two children, and now expecting a third, I understood that more would certainly be better.

The second reason, perhaps more important than the first, had to do with where I might live. When Judith and I got married, in 1970, I joined my wife in her apartment on 139th Street and Riverside Drive, not the most salubrious part of New York. One evening after the birth of our son, when we had been invited to eat with friends in Brooklyn, two of the other guests who lived a reasonably posh existence in Riverdale volunteered to give us a lift in their car. We met them in front of our building on 139th Street. The wife was stunned. Clearly she'd never imagined that people with whom she was going to have dinner could possibly call this home. She struggled for a few minutes as we sped down the West Side Highway, but finally could no longer contain herself. "Why would you live in a place like this?" she suddenly blurted out. An awkward question to be sure, but one whose impetus I totally understood. The husband, a well-paid *Times* reporter, shuddered but kept driving.

The simple answer was that on an $11,000 salary, our real estate options had been limited. The Mitchell-Lama housing project, into which I had moved, designed to provide affordable accommodation for the middle-class, possessed an adequate number of (small) bedrooms—three in all—but fell drastically short on neighborhood charm. When my wife pushed our son in his carriage from our building to the university, she was forced to pass the occasional masturbator displaying his wares in a car parked on the viaduct. The solution, I recognized, once I'd been dean for a few weeks, lay with the Columbia real estate office, which owned numerous apartments around the campus. As a lowly assistant professor I knew I stood no chance of qualifying for one, but as a dean, required to be on the campus at all times of the day and night (or so I reasoned), available to students, able to solve crises, entertain faculty, interact with alumni, and the like, maybe, just maybe, I would be found worthy. A long shot, needless to say, though no harm in trying.

So when Peter offered me the position, I decided it was time to become dean—whatever that meant. We talked about salary and he asked me what I would want. I gasped, thought of the largest amount I could ever conceive earning, and declared: $20,000. He said the provost had in mind $18,000. Having never negotiated anything about money before, I reverted to what I imagined tough guys in movies would say at this moment: "Not a penny under twenty." Peter seemed satisfied and said he would speak to the provost, stressing to him how essential he felt I would be to his administration. Somehow the extra $2,000 didn't appear to upset the provost, and I instantly felt fabulously rich. The more complicated issue was the possibility of an apartment. Peter promised to do what he could but suggested that I begin by writing a letter to the provost, who controlled the disbursement of desirable Columbia housing.

I produced a lengthy, somewhat pathetic document, talking about my three children, the sacrifice I was willing to make of my budding academic career to serve the needs of the college, and other majestically maudlin appeals crafted to melt the coldest heart of the strictest bureaucrat. It didn't work. Several days later I received from his deputy a curt rejection, noting that I was at the very bottom of the list of candidates for a prime apartment, well beneath full professors, Nobel Prize winners, department chairmen, senior administrators, and almost anybody else. Should it happen, after years of faithful toil, that in the arcane system of service and status that Columbia used to assess eligibility I might have accumulated a sufficient number of points to be considered, then I might reapply. Short of that moment, however, I should not entertain fantasies about being awarded good Columbia housing.

Having entertained precisely those fantasies for several months, I flew into a rage at the cavalier dismissal of my request. I wrote back immediately, thanking my respondent for pointing that I neither needed nor deserved an apartment, and indicating that I looked forward to the time when, after my three sons had grown up and left the house, I would finally qualify for the spacious apartment I was under the mistaken impression I desperately required now. A marvel of snottiness, it hardly advanced my cause. I began to resign myself to a 139th Street future. But Peter refused to give up on me. He appealed personally to the deputy, explaining that my unpleasant correspondence did not represent me, but attested only to the stress I was under. The deputy agreed to speak to me in his office—a huge concession.

When we met I acknowledged that, as the author of what I understood he had pronounced "the nastiest letter I had ever received," I was not in the strongest position to ask for a special favor. My rueful admission struck the proper note, and the provost's callous adjutant turned out not to be callous at all but full of rich ironies and even vaguely admiring of my rhetorical achievement. He treated me with extraordinary kindness, and within several months I had been allocated a splendid Claremont Avenue apartment to add to my enormous salary as I began to learn the ways of a dean.

The Virgil who led me through the dark woods of administrative ignorance was Peter Pouncey, a young Brit Thucydides scholar, known to all and sundry as the "Pounce." Pounce and I never ceased to marvel that two people of such disparate backgrounds and upbringing—he a British Catholic born in China who'd planned on becoming a Jesuit until he fell prey to the lusts of the body, and I a nice Jewish boy from Central Park West in New York City who had wanted more than anything to play professional basketball—should instantly form a passionate, unbreakable friendship. Peter was brash, charming, brilliant, courageous, and, perhaps most important for our compatibility, wildly funny and committed to an implacably ironic view of life. A prescient wag who wrote for the *Spectator* (the campus newspaper), sensing from the beginning our spiritual oneness, immediately dubbed us "the British-Yiddish combination." We cared hugely for the all-male undergraduates in our charge, alienating many of the lugubrious administrators pervading the rest of the university, who resented our buoyant immaturity. For while we took the job seriously, we were constitutionally unable to take ourselves seriously, a condition, or perhaps even a pathology, that others can find threatening. We wanted the college to be high-spirited and feisty, and thought it appropriate to behave accordingly.

In part, this was what the distinguished senior faculty who chose Peter—we called them the oligarchs, men like Lionel Trilling, Wm. Theodore de Bary, and Fritz Stern—sought from the college deanship. Following the destructive student uprising at Columbia in 1968 (and on a lesser note, in 1970 as well), appointing a young dean who would appeal to the undergraduates might be a wise investment. If anybody could understand what the students were thinking and feeling and know how to handle any potential unhappiness, it would be the Pounce.

This was part of the explanation for his selection. The other part was more calculating. Peter was an assistant professor, without tenure, who then became a senior administrator whose official title was "dean of the faculty of Columbia College." However, it was highly unusual to have an untenured faculty member in charge of his academically more accomplished tenured colleagues. The strategy in elevating Peter to a non-tenured deanship rested on the assumption that he would feel the vulnerability of his position and would let himself be guided by the wisdom of the faculty oligarchs on all serious issues. Thus Peter would be the perfect dean: young enough and personable enough to get along well with the students, sufficiently aware of his thin academic qualifications to ensure that he would take guidance from his professorial betters.

Right on the first count, totally wrong on the second. Peter was positively the last person on earth to doubt his own abilities or to feel that he needed help to reach proper decisions. The notion that he would appreciate input from his more respectable elders represented an astonishing misreading of the text. Peter's first official act in the summer of 1972 demonstrated the kind of dean he would be. Before he left on vacation, a group of gay Columbia students pushed for the smallest of recognitions: that a portion of a residence hall lounge be designated as a gay lounge. What forty-six years later would be too inconsequential to be noticed was at the time a very unsettling request. Although the Stonewall riots had occurred three years earlier, the culture had certainly not accommodated itself to the idea of gay rights. The president of the university was opposed, the trustees were opposed, the significant senior faculty who'd put Peter in office were opposed. The only person for it, in fact (not counting the associate dean, whose support hardly mattered), was Dean Pouncey himself; he simply thought it the right thing to do. Not a political act so much as a straightforward moral one. Despite the torrent of criticism that rained down upon him, Peter refused to budge, and so Columbia's Gay Lounge, one of the earliest of its kind, came into being. Clearly the Pounce was not going to be the pliant dean the oligarchs thought they had discovered. I watched and learned, picking up lessons that wouldn't necessarily endear me to current and future presidents.

Several months after returning from his vacation, Peter had to deal with a fight that had broken out in one of the dormitories over a dispute about how loud music should be played. Not an unusual issue, to be sure, but it had taken on a certain resonance because the alleged instigator had been a roommate of the student who had shot Dean Coleman, and anything connected with that incident brought with it an additional dose of anxiety. The director of Campus Security, a former policeman, was sufficiently concerned to notify the local police precinct, which sent up a detective to confer with Peter.

ASSOCIATE DEAN

While Dean Coleman would ordinarily handle problems of dorm behavior, it was thought in this case he should be kept out of it. Peter asked me to attend the meeting. The detective's name, memorably enough, was Rosenthal; on entering he scrutinized Peter's office, generating in me the distinct sense that he was imagining where he might stash armed policemen to defend the dean when the student arrived. He began talking about the dangers that Peter could conceivably face and, indeed, suggested that Peter consider having police stationed close by.

Rosenthal had obviously seen it all—except a British dean who knew absolutely nothing about law enforcement and would under no circumstances accept protection from his own students. Peter responded by talking about the nature of the American college, the special bond between dean and undergraduates, the importance of trust, the need to ensure that students feel respected. Rosenthal had obviously never heard anything quite like it. He sat still for a moment, staring at Pouncey, gathering his wits. Then, with a marvelous world-weary cynicism, he cranked out the unsurpassable "Those are beautiful sentiments, Dean Pouncey, but you would look funny with a third nostril." Rosenthal had won the rhetorical battle, but Pouncey still refused to be guarded, even at the risk of adding a superfluous nostril.

A few days later, the student came in to discuss his behavior. With no police officers hiding behind the drapes, the meeting went smoothly. The young man claimed to understand that punching another student was no way to win an argument; we agreed that with such a new insight he could stay in the dorm. During the entire half hour we spoke I noticed that he never took his right hand out of his coat pocket, an obvious, if heavy-handed effort to remind the young deans about what had happened to Dean Coleman. The pocket, I am confident, was empty.

SCRAPS, ORTS, AND FRAGMENTS

• • • •

Without question, the hardest thing a dean can do is to inform a family that their child has committed suicide. Insulated by my associate status from having to convey this dreadful information, I never dealt directly with grief-stricken parents. Rather, I tried to bolster the dean—whose job of comforting and explaining belonged to him alone—during these times and help him get through what is an unimaginably awful experience.

My first encounter with a student suicide was also the strangest. Several months into the fall term of 1972, Peter and I learned from the police that a student had hanged himself in his fraternity room near the campus. Peter called the family. They were understandably distraught. The boy had been happy, exuberant, successful, never showing any signs of depression. The older brother, who served as the family spokesman, remained as puzzled as he was anguished: How could a boy so full of life have taken his life? How could those who were so close to him have not appreciated his suffering?

There turned out to be an answer, though not one that anybody expected. The coroner who came to inspect the body provided it. As soon as he saw the complicated way in which the boy had hanged himself and the peculiar fact that he was clad in a leather jockstrap, the coroner grasped immediately what had happened. It was not suicide at all but an effort—which had gone too far—to intensify masturbatory satisfaction by putting pressure on the carotid artery. A well-known technique among those familiar with the arcana of self-pleasuring, it brings with it a certain user's peril. He had come across many instances of this.

Peter now had a different message to convey to the brother, which in a monstrously ironic way gave his family relief. His dead brother had not been unhappy, had not intended to kill himself. He had simply wanted to maximize self-generated sexual sensations. Peter knew as little about this practice as the brother, and the two fumbled through an awkward phone call, with Peter being aware that the bizarre nature of the death somehow made it more endurable. "Mr. Pouncey," Peter remembers the brother saying, "I never heard of this before, did you?" Peter confessed he had not. The family had lost a beloved son, but at least they had been spared the added pain of a deliberate suicide.

• • • •

When Peter took the deanship in 1972, he said he would stay for four years. Four years later, when he announced that he now planned to return to the classics department, everybody wanted to know if he had been fired. Such are the public relations consequences of doing precisely what you say you will do. The students were genuinely sad to lose their entertaining, energetic Pounce, who had so successfully infused the school with his enthusiasm; the administration professed sorrow at his loss but was, I suspect, secretly pleased not to have to deal with him any longer. Youthful exuberance and an indomitable maverick spirit can go only so far in gaining friends. The question now to be resolved: Who would follow Peter? To this end—and honoring the rules of the college faculty—McGill appointed a faculty search committee to find an appropriate candidate and recommend him to the president. The committee worked throughout the second semester, examining résumés and interviewing all manner of Columbia faculty members and others, and finally settled on one name: mine.

McGill was livid. He claimed I was totally unqualified, accused the committee of trying to embarrass him (although why my nomination constituted an actual embarrassment remained murky), and said under no circumstances would he interview me. Was this

McGill doing his fabricated-rage performance or did he truly have a profound emotional response to the thought of me as dean? Unclear, but whatever his motivation, he certainly managed to shatter the committee's confidence in the search it had conducted in good faith, imagining that the president would be pleased with the final choice, over which it had labored so diligently. Psychologist McGill, however, knew exactly what he was doing. Having assailed the members for their dreadful failure in coming up with someone so patently unacceptable, making them all question their self-worth, he then displayed his flexibility and gratitude for their efforts by agreeing to speak to me. They didn't get it right, but in his benevolent authority he would in fact be willing to consider the candidate they had found.

Soon I was summoned to his office for what clearly was to be a fake interview, designed to show that he took their recommendation seriously. It turned out that he actually did have reason to be unhappy with me beyond my initial offense in trying to clarify the university's position about the shooting of deans. I had forgotten that several years later I had indeed offended the president over his negotiations with the army to bring the ROTC program back to campus. Following the disturbances of 1968, Columbia had severed connection with its ROTC units. Student interest in the program—most particularly in the scholarship money involved—had later started up, and by the mid-seventies I had begun to hear rumors that talks between the army and McGill were taking place. When the *Daily Spectator* called me to ask my opinion about ROTC coming back, I behaved in my usual intemperate manner, asserting that as this was a college matter, it was outrageous that the college had not been consulted and, furthermore, remarked that the president had no right to pursue unilateral discussions. It never occurred to me that associate deans ought not to be quite so cavalier in publicly attacking the president.

If I had ceased to dwell on my affront, McGill had certainly not forgotten. As soon as we sat down, he immediately launched into a virulent assault on my unacceptable behavior in criticizing him. I had no way to defend myself—my guilt was both explicit and egregious—and I could only sit there quietly as he savaged me. When he slowed down I agreed that I had acted improperly but, struggling for a response that I thought demonstrated my maturity, added that surely he couldn't hold that single incident against my entire candidacy.

"No, no," he assured me, waving away such a silly thought (though not for a moment relinquishing the idea), and then went on to engage me in talk about the college. The interview was a charade, of course, as he had not the slightest interest in me or my thoughts about undergraduate life. Its sole purpose was to prove to the committee his commitment to respect the search process. Our chat was amiable enough; McGill could be charming when he wanted to. We discussed the odd timing: he had to fill not only the college deanship but also that of the School of General Studies, the adult division of the university, whose associate dean, Ward Dennis, was also the prime candidate for the position. "He can't shine your shoes intellectually—he'll never get it," McGill confided in me, two weeks before appointing Dennis dean of General Studies.

As McGill had obviously understood, the committee was pleased that he had consented to our talk. And they were all positively ecstatic when he let them know that he was so delighted with their choice that he wanted to interview me again. By this time they could hardly argue that the president had not honored their efforts. Having softened them up through his anger, he earned their approbation by pretending to take their nominee seriously.

Our second conversation took place on a late Saturday morning in the presidential mansion, built for Nicholas Murray Butler in

1912. McGill couldn't have been friendlier. He met me wearing a casual polo shirt, took me, in the house's personal elevator, to the fourth-floor sitting room, and ordered up a gin and tonic from his butler. Unlike during our previous meeting, there was no berating, no attempt to diminish. He spoke about what it was like to be president, about the cost to his family from the obligations of the job. He even acknowledged that the burdens of fundraising could interfere with one's sex life—a confession I found so intimate that I resolved never to tell anyone, until I heard from a professor in the philosophy department that he had revealed this same truth at a faculty meeting. In short, a totally pleasant interaction, though I knew that it had nothing to do with my becoming the dean.

McGill had extricated himself from a difficult political situation with considerable skill. He had convinced the committee that he realized they had found an admirable man with many virtues, and that if I wasn't exactly what he wanted, the committee was not at fault. They had worked hard and should be commended. That done, McGill was free to send them back to continue the hunt.

In the meantime, he and the provost would appoint an acting dean who could be counted on to cause no trouble. The choice was Robert Belknap, a professor of Slavic languages and a college loyalist who had spent a year serving in the Dean of Students Office some time before. Tall and ungainly, wreathed in personal awkwardness, he always reminded me a bit of Ichabod Crane. A beloved teacher of Dostoevsky and Tolstoy, he was eager to trade in his academic credentials to become the permanent dean of Columbia College. He saw the acting deanship as a miraculous route to a position for which no faculty search committee would ever consider him. He would do whatever the provost, Ted de Bary, who was closer to him than McGill, wanted him to do if it would gain him the prize.

ASSOCIATE DEAN

The first thing de Bary apparently asked him to do was get rid of me. I learned this when I went on vacation to Calabria, several weeks after Belknap's appointment. I called my secretary from a hot, wasp-filled phone booth on the beach to see how the search was proceeding, only to discover from her that Belknap had just announced my resignation. This was news to me, as well as to various faculty friends who knew I had done no such thing. Needless to say I was shocked, but I came up with what I thought was a superb response: "Tell Bob I would never do that to him," I instructed Sandy. "I will certainly see him when I return." Professorial colleagues meanwhile trooped into Bob's office, requiring him to issue a statement that it had all been a misunderstanding and that I remained the associate dean.

While Belknap had delivered himself of the lie, I had no doubt that de Bary had come up with the idea. He had never liked any part of the British-Yiddish combination, and with the voluntary departure of the British portion, he had clearly jumped at the opportunity to clear out the other toxic half. I certainly had reasons to be nervous about my future, but I didn't think Belknap would actually be willing to fire me—I had significant faculty support and, after all, was the search committee's candidate for dean—and in any case he had no grounds to think we couldn't work harmoniously together.

We had a congenial discussion in his office when I returned. I think I convinced him that having worked at the job for four years I could probably be helpful to him, and that he could trust me to do my best to make good decisions. He projected relief, suggesting he would see how things developed. I said I was confident we would get along. Then, as I headed for the door, I turned and rather overly dramatically, I am forced to admit, uttered a good, tough-sounding line: "Bob, I just want to let you know that I have no intention of resigning." He nodded in mute understanding; I had made clear that I wouldn't go easily or quietly.

While I could never make de Bary find me acceptable, Belknap had no difficulties with me. I did what he asked and tried to provide the social polish he so sorely lacked. When, several months into the fall term, a small fire broke out in one of the dormitories, causing minor injuries to a few students, Bob sought to rush a letter into print for the involved parents that would fully account for what happened and calm their anxieties about their children. Bob's eagerness to get it right produced a document whose tone was bizarrely out of control. A fire occurred in one of the lounges, his letter (correctly) noted; it then went on to state (completely incorrectly) that one of the students was hideously burned—though fortunately he would recover. I tried to point out that if the aim of the letter was to make parents think everything was all right, claiming, when it wasn't even true, that a student had been "hideously burned" was not the best way to explain what had happened. He agreed. Later I told a dean of the graduate school how I had been editing Bob's letters and assorted communications with faculty and alumni in an effort to make them more readable. He was not a fan of Belknap's and had one word for me: "Don't." I continued, however, to do what I could with his prose.

As the fall semester moved on, the search committee continued their labors. They became particularly interested in Arnold Collery, an economics professor at Amherst who had spent a year as acting dean of the college. It gradually became clear that Collery was their choice. Despite his impressive qualifications, the provost did not share the committee's enthusiasm for Collery. Instead he had firmly decided on Belknap as his candidate, less for any administrative virtues he might have possessed than for the fact that with Bob as dean the provost knew he would effectively be running the college.

ASSOCIATE DEAN

Having fought with the Pounce over budgets, admissions, housing, and more or less everything else during the course of four years, de Bary wanted to make sure he would no longer encounter any administrative opposition. Dean Belknap could guarantee that.

The search committee, unfortunately, had no intention of nominating him, so if de Bary could not persuade them to prefer Belknap to Collery, he would have to find some way to discourage Collery from coming. He formulated a brilliantly original tactic, writing a long, unpleasant letter to McGill, enumerating in great detail all of Collery's shortcomings and emphasizing the many different ways he would inevitably fail as dean, and then sending a copy to Collery himself. Receiving a letter from the provost to the president indicating how unsuitable you are for the position you thought you wanted is an odd experience, and Collery admitted to being dumbfounded by it. But he had been at Amherst for more than twenty years and was ready for a move to the city. He was also—happily—stubborn. One weird provostial communication could not dissuade him from coming to New York.

With Collery still remaining interested in the job, de Bary had to go to his backup strategy. Collery was a tenured professor at Amherst, and de Bary knew he would not come to Columbia unless he had similar status in our economics department. If he were determined to accept the deanship despite having received his dreadful letter, denying him tenure would most assuredly keep him away. At the time, tenure at Columbia was determined by an ad hoc committee composed of five faculty members from outside the candidate's department. As the senior administrator in charge of the ad hoc process, de Bary accordingly set about appointing a committee that would do his bidding, finding academic reasons to prevent Collery from getting tenure. One obvious way to attempt this would be to establish a committee of such fierce distinction that nobody could measure up. But de Bary was wilier than that. He didn't want to leave it to chance, to eminent, strong-minded scholars who didn't necessarily care what the provost had in mind. He sought instead to put together a group of lesser professorial lights, men unwilling to stand up against authority, whom he could almost certainly coerce to vote no.

The search committee, meanwhile, had been working for nearly a year and had long since run out of patience with McGill. They felt they had taken their mandate seriously, had successfully negotiated the trauma of my candidacy, and had now found in Arnold Collery a qualified, experienced person who would be a fine dean. From their point of view there was no reason to consider anybody else and certainly no grounds for meddling with his tenure in order to cause him not to accept the offer that should properly be his. At a meeting with McGill, the chairman, Rufus Mathewson, a Slavic department colleague of Belknap's, told him that the committee had agreed that if there were any more delays or efforts at interference they would go public with the whole convoluted procedure, something neither the president nor the provost would appreciate. McGill should put an end to the mess, Mathewson suggested, award Collery tenure, as he had the power to do, and confer the deanship upon him. McGill had no particular interest in Belknap—or even Collery, for that matter. He was, however, deeply interested in peace, and in not having the search committee he'd appointed be subverted by the obsessions of the provost. He consented, and Arnold Collery shortly became the eleventh dean of Columbia College.

Encouraged by de Bary's support, Belknap continued to believe the provost could make his deanship happen. He wanted it too badly to be able to read any of the signs. Several days after everybody in our office knew that Collery had been chosen, Belknap still thought he had a chance. The president's indifference to Belknap could not have been more flagrantly displayed than when he informed him of his decision: he sent him a brief note through the campus mail, not even bothering with the decency of a phone call. Belknap had believed in the power of the provost, but it had failed him.

• • • •

Preparing for the arrival of women in the fall of '83, we knew we had to repair John Jay Hall, the decaying dormitory where most of the first-year women would be housed. Grim conditions that were deemed acceptable for men (though of course they weren't) would not be for women. If coeducation was to be successful, or so we argued vehemently to the administration, the students had to be properly housed.

It was hard to disagree, and no one did. Budget and personnel were assigned to guarantee that when parents brought their sons and daughters to campus they would be pleased with the accommodations we had provided. Committees were set up to oversee the work, gigantic spreadsheets were established to enable us to track our progress, and a foreman—whose name, appropriately enough, was Forman—was even put in charge, to ensure specific accountability. We met throughout the summer, receiving reports on how far we had come and how far we had to go. We were all nervous, but foreman Forman assured us we were on schedule.

One week before the students were due, we had our last meeting. We all turned up except Mr. Forman, who had apparently forgotten. Looking out the window of the office in which we were gathering, I saw him ambling by. "Look, there he is!" I shouted, and the director of university housing ran out and grabbed him. "The kids are coming in a week," I said. "Are things all right?"

"Everything is fine," he replied. "A few little problems, but nothing serious."

"What are they?" I asked.

"Well, on two floors (I forget which), the men's and women's toilets have no stalls."

I was scarcely able to believe what I was hearing. "You mean people will be sitting thigh to thigh like in the army?"

He nodded. My rage was such that I found it hard to speak. I tried to remain sane enough to point out that this was not what students and their parents expected when they came to Columbia and that such an arrangement was entirely and absolutely unacceptable. He remained unperturbed, seemingly puzzled by my anger. "OK," he said, then finally acknowledged that he could build some temporary wooden stalls while awaiting the permanent ones—for the girls, but not for the guys. They would simply have to manage until the permanent ones arrived. At this point I am afraid I lost it and started shouting that the men required the same temporary stalls as the women. He grudgingly allowed that he would take care of it.

"Anything else?" I inquired, incredulous that I was having this conversation with the very man whose job it was to make sure that the new students had a happy and welcoming experience at Columbia.

There are some rooms, he mentioned (he had forgotten the number, perhaps five or six), that don't yet have doors.

I received this news calmly, assuming that the rooms would remain unoccupied until the doors arrived. No, he assured me, students will be in them.

Again I struggled to hold myself together. "You mean students are going to arrive with their typewriters, stereos, and assorted precious belongings and not be able to store them safely behind a closed door? I tried to comprehend Mr. Forman, trying to comprehend how information that made me crazy didn't seem to bother him in the least. Would it be possible, I thought, that people in charge of overseeing undergraduate living renovations at Harvard, Yale, and Princeton would take the same relaxed view of rooms without doors and toilets without stalls? I doubted it.

At least there was no one to take his side, and after some more browbeating, he agreed to build temporary doors. A week later, the first coeducational class at Columbia College moved in without incident.

The Kovner Bowl

The first American collegiate football "bowl" game, played in 1902, during which Michigan beat Stanford, 49–0, was not exactly a bowl game. It was sponsored by the California Tournament of Roses Association and technically should be thought of as an "East-West Tournament football game." The association continued to underwrite these annual contests until, in 1923, the game moved into the newly finished Rose Bowl Stadium, permanently rooting itself in this distinguished venue and taking on the title of the "Rose Bowl Game." Gradually other parts of the country began to understand the economic and public relations virtues of hosting high-profile football games, and bowls started to metastasize across the nation: the well-known ones—Orange, Cotton, Sun, Gator, Fiesta, Sugar—and those of lesser visibility: Chick-fil-A, Liberty, Famous Idaho Potato, Belk, Mineral Water, Pioneer, Oyster, Soup, and Egg, among others, generally played from late in December through the first two weeks in January. Total? Approximately forty-two, currently, not counting a relative latecomer, the professional Super Bowl, the most lavishly staged of them all, with television commercials during this extravagant event costing somewhere in the millions for thirty-second spots. And should you (properly) conclude that football bowl games are at least as American as apple pie, you should at the same time recognize that bowl games—sometimes football, sometimes soccer—have popped up around the world, in Germany, Finland, Japan, Great Britain, Ireland, Brazil, and Israel, among other countries. Bowls, in short, are everywhere.

While I can appreciate that, with very few exceptions, no one has ever heard of the Kovner Bowl, the mere fact that it's not a household name is no reason to continue to condemn it to the conspiracy of silence. Any athletic contest played over a period of twenty nearly consecutive years—with only several minor interruptions—on the same day (Thanksgiving Saturday), at the same time (ten a.m.), with three of the six participants the same, on the same scruffy field in Central Park (in front of the Eighty-sixth Street basketball courts) deserves at least some recognition. Thirty-nine years since the last pass was thrown, it is time to celebrate the history of the Kovner Bowl.

Named for the cousins Kovner (not to be confused with the Brothers Karamazov), two of the game's three founding fathers (I was the third), it was first played in 1957. Finding ourselves in New York to have Thanksgiving dinners with our families, Tony, Victor, and I recognized the opportunity for some pleasurable exercise afforded by a free Saturday morning. We agreed that a three-man touch football game would be the perfect activity to fill the time. Tony and Victor would recruit their third teammate, I would round up my two, and we would duke it out in Central Park. It was not necessary to specify that in forming our squads we had to adhere to the principle of comparable athletic mediocrity. No former college football players. No high school track stars. Intense commitment to winning, of course, was assumed, as long as no one possessed any sizable physical advantages. Since I had two draft choices to the cousins Kovner's one, I had to be particularly honest in my choices, careful to eschew speed and grace in favor of determined plodding. I also had a usable football. Even more important, I had a pin to inflate it. Ball and pin lasted throughout all the years of our bitter competition.

Several phone calls filled out our rosters, and on Saturday morning we six assembled at the entrance to the park to seek an available location. The field we settled on was sufficiently grassless and desiccated that no one else ever thought to play there. It remained uncontestedly the site of the Kovner Bowl for the next twenty years.

The rules were simple and standard for makeshift touch football games such as ours. No blocking, count to "five Mississippi" before rushing across the line of scrimmage, no forward passing once you crossed the line. Passes instead of punts and kickoffs. Four downs for each team. If no touchdown is scored, the ball shifts to the other side. We began with an actual ticking clock to time two halves of forty or forty-five minutes each. The official timekeeper at the start was Victor's sister, Amy. After several years, however, it became increasingly clear to me that family pressure had introduced a touch of corruption into the supervision of the game clock: when the Kovners were ahead, the game mysteriously seemed to speed up, slowing down when they were behind. I was forced to file a complaint with the rules committee, and while no admission of guilt was actually forthcoming, we all agreed that the integrity of the game would best be protected by switching from a clock to a set number of plays for each half, which both teams could monitor. Following this resolution, all proceeded smoothly. The only other major (or, for that matter, minor) adjustment occurred when we eliminated the pass-offs, requiring running down the field, that began each half, in favor of one team simply starting by taking the ball out on what was more or less the twenty-yard line. Less running was seen to be a virtue, lightening the stress on increasingly creaky legs.

THE KOVNER BOWL

The first game ended in a tie, one of only three. Although team Kovner had the advantage of a core of two players who knew each other's moves and shared strategy, they suffered under the obligation of having to enlist assorted brothers-in-law and other family members to fill out their squad, some of whom were not American and understood little about football, tackle or touch. I, on the other hand, had no such constraints in building a team. While I concentrated on high school and college friends, I did in fact make the single most brilliant choice in the long history of the Kovner Bowl. I billed him as my mystery player, and brought him to a game in the early 1980s clad in a Pooh Bear mask. Tony loved the idea that he didn't know his identity, as I had him keep the mask on until the game was about to begin. It was my stepson Stephen, who had begun his bowl experience as a young spectator and was now old enough and athletic enough to be a player. He performed well and helped us win. Tony thought it an inspired selection.

The result of the occasional Kovner family coercion was a mild disparity in the talent level, particularly when the cousins Kovner were saddled with employing well-meaning but athletically compromised participants. According to archivist Tony, when the game was disbanded in 1983, in recognition of encroaching old age and increasing out of shapeness, the Rosenthals were leading the Kovners, 10–5. (The bowl was not held from 1974 through 1980 for reasons no one is entirely clear about, perhaps having to do with Tony being out of the city.)

The Kovner Bowl, of course, was indifferent to the vagaries of weather. Records kept by our archivist indicate it generally took place under fair conditions, though three times it rained and twice was notably cold. Three games received weather question marks, but none was ever canceled for inclemencies. One unexpected injury caused a cancellation in 1966. We were warming up on the field before the game when I threw a long, looping pass to Victor, who failed to use his hands to catch the ball, instead clutching it to his midriff. Although I was not known for the power of my arm, the football delivered a sufficient blow to his stomach to require him to be carried from the field and carted off to one of the two hospitals his father owned. Fortunately, he was not seriously hurt, but we were all stunned and frustrated at the absence of our game.

The ritual of the Kovner Bowl generated its own weird brand of competitiveness, and I have to confess that as ridiculous as I understood it to be, I really wanted to win each year. It wasn't a casual encounter for me. Winning mattered. I say this to account for what I consider perhaps my lowest moment in the bowl's history, my rage at one of my teammates for costing me a defeat.

It was in the early 1980s, the last play of a tied game. The Kovners were more or less on our goal line. Long years of playing against them had led me to know exactly what they would do, as they really had only one strategy. I called a time-out and summoned my two teammates. "Here is what will happen," I explained. "Victor and Tony will run out and cross, hoping to get us tangled up while guarding them. So all we have to do is not go with them, but simply play to the outside, switching men as they cross the field. Tony, my man, will then run into you," I pointed out to Jody, a former Columbia student. "And Victor, your man, will become mine. The big thing is to remember not to cross with them but just play to the outside. So you will end by guarding Tony and I will be on Victor. OK?"

Jody assured me that he got it. The play then began. They crossed, I waited for Victor to come to me, then suddenly, with enormous horror, I realized that Jody was standing next to Victor and me, leaving Tony totally unguarded on the other side of the field. I screamed, but to no avail. The pass was thrown, Tony easily caught it, we lost.

Jody later said he had never seen such a terrible look on my face as I digested what had happened. I couldn't believe what he had done; nor could I finally believe what I had done, flying into a rage at a good friend who had come out to play a silly game of touch football in the park with me. We both felt awful. As reprehensible as I found my angry behavior, however, I could never comprehend why he did not stay on the outside, as I had instructed him.

My Almost Club Life

I was never a joiner. No Boy Scouts, no youth groups, no book clubs, no after-school organizations of any sort. Plenty of athletics, especially basketball, but being on a team constituted an entirely different kind of affiliation from being a club member. I am not sure why, but I just found joining anything to be difficult. When I got to Harvard, someone told me I had a good voice and should think about the radio station. I went to the introductory meeting and lasted two days until I stopped going.

In my junior year I decided to join the Hasty Pudding Club, billed as the oldest social club in America, founded in 1795. But since it had no admission requirements and accepted all comers, it couldn't be thought of as exactly a club. I don't remember ever talking to anybody there. My sole activity in the clubhouse was on occasion to munch a small dish of popcorn with a beer. The Pudding bore no resemblance to Harvard's exclusive and elegant "final" clubs, like the Porcellian or the Fly, which would not consider admitting pedestrian types like me no matter how hard I tried.

That is how I remained for the next thirty or so years, happily unconnected, leading my full urban-academic life, belonging nowhere—not even the Harvard or Columbia clubs—despite their endless efforts to enroll me. Until my good friend Edward Said, some twenty-five years ago, decided it might be fun if I joined him as a member of the Century Club (technically the Century Association, though few people bothered to make that distinction). There were dinners, musical evenings, and lectures, not to mention a good place for a drink if you were in midtown. "You should join, Michael," he exhorted me. "It will add to the pleasures of the city." Edward was a persuasive man, and though I had never thought about becoming a "Centurion," as members are entitled to refer to themselves, I said I would consider it.

Of the many private clubs available in New York, the Century is unique in its ostensible commitment to achievement in literature and the fine arts. Founded in 1847 and called the Century after its first hundred members (at this time numbering more than two thousand), it prides itself on the creative accomplishments of its members. The list of United States presidents (eight), Supreme Court justices (ten), cabinet officials (forty-three), and Nobel Prize winners (twenty-nine) suggests that the Century is not entirely indifferent to power and worldly status, but it maintains a warm spot for those who write, paint, or compose. Being admitted confers a distinction in itself, regardless of the good times membership affords. Mark Twain thought of it as the "most unspeakably respectable club in the United States."

Although there were certainly other things to do with one's money, I could see no downside to joining. Even if I wouldn't likely hang around Forty-third Street for a daily martini, as some people did, I would still belong, which was sort of the point in any case. I told Edward he should do whatever had to be done to start the nominating process. I rounded up the requisite number of supporting letters from members, spoke to those whom Edward directed me to speak to, had lunch with representatives of the admissions committee, and waited to hear the good news. Given the fact that I had written several books, been awarded several prestigious fellowships, and, by my own strict standards, was capable, under duress, of humor and charm, I thought of myself as a perfect candidate to become a Centurion. So when Edward called me several days after my admissions lunch to inform me I had been rejected, I assumed he was joking.

"Come on, Edward, you can't be serious," I retorted. "I was at the top of my game at the lunch and got along well with the interviewers. They couldn't possibly have decided against me." Edward then explained that the rules of the Century permit a single objection on the part of any member, not necessarily anybody officially connected to the admissions process, to be enough to sink a nomination. People liked me and I had sufficient qualifications, Edward insisted, but one person was opposed and that was it.

All negative decisions are kept in strictest confidence at the Century, making it difficult for anyone to track down the source responsible for a blackball, but Edward had his ways and eventually determined that a Columbia dean whom I had treated dismissively at some college meeting had exacted his revenge by preventing me from joining. Fair enough, I thought, as I had in fact been mildly stern with him on several occasions, though going to the trouble of keeping me out of his august club did seem a bit much. On the other hand, I reflected, having such a power must surely be one of the reasons to be a member in the first place.

So I was not going to be a Centurion after all. A surprise, as I had never imagined that I might not be admitted. I can't say I was particularly dismayed, membership having never risen to a priority in my life. While I was friendly with several dozen members of the club, I was now one of only two I knew who had been turned down. An achievement of a sort, I thought.

I remained happily clubless, not for a moment lamenting that my visits to the club were always as an invited guest rather than a belonging member.

Approximately a dozen years ago two friends came to the same conclusion that Edward had reached: the Century would be exactly right for me and I should join. I explained that I had already tried that and failed. I wasn't especially interested in reapplying. They persisted. The procedure has changed, they pointed out. No longer can one secret veto terminate a candidate. It's an admissions committee decision, and the process is open. Besides, several of your strong supporters, they told me, are on the committee, so there really isn't an issue. I emphasized that while I was essentially neutral on the subject of joining, I really wanted to avoid being rejected a second time. If once could be taken as a peculiar kind of achievement, twice had no discernible appeal attached to it. I did not want to be arguably the only person in the history of the club to have managed two successive failures.

My friends claimed they understood and contended that it couldn't possibly happen. Our good-natured disagreement continued on for a number of weeks, until I finally capitulated, convinced that the application process could only end positively. My two instigators did not want to do the legwork required of sponsors, however, and enlisted a third friend to take over those responsibilities. I solicited new letters, spoke to new people. Nothing seemed to be happening, but I was not perturbed since I had been assured everything was in place. My sponsor then informed me that someone I knew reasonably well who was a member of the admissions committee wanted to meet with the two of us for a drink. I thought this odd, as I had known her for a couple of years and couldn't imagine what she might expect to learn from talking to me now. But if that was what she wanted, fine. I shared my perplexity with Ric, my sponsor, but he dismissed my concerns and encouraged me to have one of the club's famous martinis and relax.

The three of us came together, and everything was friendly if a bit awkward, as I couldn't figure out what she wanted to know that she didn't already know. At the start of our conversation I remembered that she had recently been teaching at Union College, in Schenectady, and asked what seemed like a perfectly reasonable question: Was she still there? She replied softly—and, I thought, a bit coldly—that she was teaching at Columbia, in the School of the Arts. "Oh, great," I said, though there was no way I would necessarily know that. I had the distinct feeling, however, that it was expected that I should.

Realizing that I had started off badly, I attempted to repair things by revealing that I was aware that she had a growing reputation as a biographer. "Are you giving a course in biography?" I inquired, hoping to cover my error in not knowing where she was currently teaching. Big mistake, as she apparently took this comment as an attempt to demean her gifts as an author. "No, I teach a course in nonfiction writing," she tartly responded, making it clear that she chose not to be categorized as the practitioner of a low-end genre such as biography. Having no such view about the art of biography myself, I don't know how I could have understood this.

The interview dragged on painfully; I never solved the problem of what she wanted to know. I sipped my martini and ate my cashews, working at staying civil and accessible. I told Ric as I left that I didn't think it had gone well, but he scoffed at my judgment, claiming it was fine and didn't matter anyway.

I heard nothing from the club for several months. Then I got a call informing me that the admissions committee wanted to have a group interview with five or six members (not including my biographical colleague) at the club. "And one more thing," I was told. "Don't let it be all about you. Ask about the lives of those who show up for the discussion." Pondering the meaning of this helpful hint, I concluded it must have stemmed from another failure of mine at the earlier meeting. Sure enough, it later emerged that in addition to my ignorance as to where she taught and what she taught, I had neglected to inquire about the health of her husband. Absolutely guilty on that count I had to admit, though it had never occurred to me that posing the perfunctory question about how he was feeling was expected of me. And as I noted (to myself only), she hadn't wondered about Judy's well-being, either.

Whatever reservations the committee might have been sharing about me, the meeting was completely congenial. My character, I thought, emerged unscathed from the conversation, and I made sure to inquire about everyone's personal lives and the life of the club. I enjoyed the conversation and felt they did as well.

Still, nothing happened. Finally, almost a month later, something did happen: I was rejected, becoming that very loathsome thing I had most wanted to avoid, a two-time failure. My adversary had successfully, even heroically resisted the committee's enthusiasm for me. She stood alone against them all—and won. During the discussion at one point, I learned, she asked my greatest supporter to leave the room so that she could feel more comfortable vilifying me. Sadly, my friend honored this preposterous request.

While I can understand the indomitable nature of her antipathy, no one was capable of explaining its content. I had never been unpleasant to her or done her harm, discounting my most recent sin of not appreciating that she was teaching at Columbia. As far as I knew, I was totally innocent of wrongdoing. Various schemes were apparently discussed by the committee to allow my candidacy to go forward in the face of her staunch resistance, but because they all seemed to involve manipulating the Century's transparent procedures, it was decided that the wiser course was simply to forgo the struggle on my behalf and move on. I told my Century friends who had encouraged my second effort that I would prefer it if no one tried to entice me into a third attempt.

Clearly I was not destined to be a Centurion, even if I produced a Pulitzer Prize–winning symphony. Two rejections were quite enough. I would have to manage without the club's fabled martinis.

Which I certainly did, and with no sense of loss. I continued to teach and continued to explore new scholarly projects, though none seemed quite right. A phone call from a friend in the early 1990s changed all of that. "Let's have lunch," she said. "I have the perfect book for you to do." That perfect book turned out to be a biography of Nicholas Murray Butler, Columbia's president from 1902 to 1945, and one of this country's most extraordinary characters, called by the *New York Times* in 1937 "Prime Minister of the Republic of the Intellect." My friend Mary had noticed that the control over Butler's papers in Columbia's rare book and manuscript collection had just been lifted; she insisted this was the book I had to write. I agreed. Some 600 boxes of papers, 144 volumes of clippings, and countless other sources condemned me to a dozen years in the rare book library. I finally stumbled out with my five hundred pages on Butler's life, *Nicholas Miraculous*.

During the final years of my voluntary incarceration in the library, one of the librarians who had supplied me with Butler materials asked if I would be interested in talking to members of the Lotos

Club about Butler's life. Butler loved his multiple club affiliations, but he particularly loved the Lotos, which he joined in 1915 and became president of in 1923. His affection for the club and its distinguished membership led him to write the lyrics for a song entitled "Lotos Land," faithfully performed by the Lotosians before every official dinner.

The Lotos couldn't provide a stipend for the talk, I was told, but it would bring with it a year's free membership and use of the clubhouse facilities. If after a year I was contemplating joining, I would be more or less guaranteed admission. And my status as an academic also meant I would receive an enormous discount on the cost.

All for discussing Butler's virtues for a half hour while the members ate their lunches, I went ahead with the arrangements. Following the talk, I asked a club official when my privileges would begin. He looked puzzled. "Tonight if you would like," he responded. That seemed happily prompt, I thought. This could be fun. And so it was. I had a number of dinners with good food served by white-gloved waiters; surprised my wife with the unexpected arrival of my eldest son and his partner as we were having drinks in front of the fireplace, in which real logs were burning; and enjoyed the general aura of well-being that elegant clubhouses on East Sixty-sixth Street off Fifth Avenue have the power to confer. I didn't really belong, of course, I just could pretend for a year, but I did have a sense of what had soothed Butler's soul, prompting him to write the lyrics for "Lotos Land."

My only behavioral blunder occurred one evening when I found myself on the East Side and thought it would be classy to stop in at "my club" for dinner with my wife. I understood that the dress code required a jacket and tie, so I arrived properly prepared. I went to the desk to find out about the possibility of a table. The manager, or whoever was staffing the desk, picked up the phone to inquire, then let me know there was nothing available. I thought it strange that she didn't actually say anything but just appeared to listen. I then asked if I could I just have a drink in the lounge, since I wasn't sure how to proceed. She looked at me rather unpleasantly and pointed out that as I was wearing jeans it wouldn't be appropriate for me to be in the club at all. I apologized profusely, explaining that while I knew about the necessity of jacket and tie, I hadn't realized that jeans were forbidden. I left in some disgrace, and made sure to never enter the building again without my gray flannels.

My wife and I enjoyed our (occasional) club dinners, and as my temporary tenure approached its end, I thought I should consider becoming an authentic member. Friends mostly laughed at the idea, but with my substantial academic discount I could see no reason not to. I made them promise that if I invited them for dinner, they would come. They all agreed.

The admission process was not unlike that of the Century: several supporting letters, a few one-on-one interviews, and finally a meeting with the entire admissions committee. Everything went well. Several weeks later I received a nice note welcoming me, a list of associated clubs in Europe and England where I could stay when traveling, and an invitation to the dinner for new members. Then a surprise: a statement of how much I owed for my first year's dues. Clearly a mistake, as it was literally ten times what I had anticipated, given my academic status.

I called the appropriate office to notify them that an error had been made. I was told that the person in charge of billing issues would call me. He turned out to be a medical malpractice lawyer, precisely the kind of lawyer with whom I least wanted to discuss how much I owed. When he contacted me, I explained in all innocence that I believed my statement had to be incorrect. I had been told from the time I had been approached about speaking at the club that if I wanted to join I would be charged a special academic rate. And who could be more of an academic than someone who had spent his entire life after college as a graduate student, professor, and university administrator?

Clearly a simple mistake, then. He seemed not to see it that way, however, and began asking me about the sources of my income, the nature of my investments, and other issues concerning my financial condition—issues that to my mind had nothing to do with the unadorned fact that I was the purest instance of a one hundred percent academic that I knew. If I didn't qualify for a special academic rate, I suggested, nobody could. He indicated that we would have to talk more about this, as it was more complicated than I appreciated.

Thinking about the paradox of how I could simultaneously be a full-time academic but not qualify as one according to club rules, I suddenly understood the problem: it was not some arcane view of the meaning of "academic" so much as a matter of my income. In Lotos Land, "academic" had nothing to do with what I did and everything with the size of my pension. I apparently did not fit the profile of the needy academic awarded special dispensation to frolic with his tonier club colleagues. I might have been a legitimate professor, but I was not the appropriately poor kind the Lotos sought to help diversify its membership. I could see the narrative shaping up: "Rosenthal is trying to screw a discount out of us, but we found him out." This was not a controversy I could win. Even if I won I would be a loser.

I told Judy I had to terminate my application, and she agreed. I wrote a note stating that while I could not comprehend by what bizarre logic I fell outside their academic category, I surely didn't want to argue or put them to any trouble. I thanked them for all they had done. I have never ceased relishing the irony of voluntarily withdrawing from a club that had actually accepted me after my two previous rejections. Little did I imagine that nibbling popcorn as an undergraduate at the Hasty Pudding in 1957 would constitute my most gratifying—and my solitary—club experience.

Should We Meet Today?

Time was running out and I had made not an iota of progress in the critical project I had been working on for several months. It was April 1969. I was an instructor in the English department at Columbia College, teaching three consecutive hours on Mondays, Wednesdays, and Fridays, from ten a.m. to one p.m. These details may seem unimportant but they're not, for they account for the existence of the project. Because I taught for three hours in a row, I felt I needed a late breakfast to keep my energy level up through the three classes. The best place for that was John Jay Hall, on the campus, where one could grab some scrambled eggs and sit at a refectory table in the dining room without being disturbed. Which was where I would generally be found around nine o'clock in the morning, eating my eggs and mulling over the material shortly to be presented to the students.

A perfect situation for pre-class preparation, with only one problem. Early in the semester, as I scanned the vastness of the dining room for a good place to sit, my eye fell upon what I thought was a marvelously attractive woman sipping coffee and studying some kind of text. Returning several times a week for my sustaining breakfasts, I noticed that, more often than not, she was there as well. I looked and I fantasized, rendering the class preparation of decidedly secondary importance. Seeing her became the real quest of my John Jay attendance. But, of course, looking and fantasizing was hardly the point. If I wanted to meet her, I would have to do something dramatic, like saying hello. And this was difficult, if not actually impossible for me. Picking up desirable women (of which daring to speak to this one certainly qualified as a species of such behavior) was never my strong suit. I had gone through a respectable number of girlfriends, but almost all had been introduced to me in one way or another, either at parties or as blind dates. Some deep-rooted lack of confidence prevented me from breaking free of the bonds of inhibition to casually engage women I didn't know. Once I met them I was fine, but meeting them was not easy.

My weekly morning failures in the spring of '69 generated lots of material for my afternoon psychoanalytic sessions, now in their fifth year, if they didn't produce any solutions. Short of accompanying me to John Jay to introduce me to the object of my desire, I don't know what my analyst could have done. I knew he was rooting for me, but no amount of free-associating and digging into my neurotic blocks managed to effect my liberation. While I could lament my sorry condition with some eloquence in his office, that seemed all I could do. I still couldn't get myself to initiate a conversation. Nor could I imagine that she noticed me looking at her.

Meanwhile, I was distinctly aware that the school year was coming to an end. As I had concluded that she had to be a graduate student, this added a dose of panic to my breakfast paralysis. For once school was over, I understood, she would no longer appear and the opportunity would be lost. In pathetic response to this insight, I moved my refectory table seat ever closer to wherever she sat, though my silence remained unbroken. Finally, at the end of April, on a Friday, I perched myself directly behind her and stared at her back, pondering what I might say. I couldn't possibly be sitting closer to her. If she wasn't careful, she might actually bump into me if she got up first. This had to be it.

After a semester of silent agonizing about how I might contrive to meet her, the moment suddenly presented itself. She stood up, turned around, and there I was, silent as ever, but now flashing the biggest, warmest smile I could fashion. Five and a half years of analysis in the making. If it wasn't exactly the speech I sought, it was at least a demonstrable invitation of sorts. She took it all in, staring down at me, smiling up at her. Her first words—the first words between us—were cool, incisive, magnificent: "Shall we meet today, or should we wait a little longer?" I couldn't have asked for anything more. She was wry, she understood, and, above all, she had noticed me noticing her and had even been intrigued by it. In a stroke the semester's fantasizing had been fulfilled. While I am not sure it could technically count as a pickup, as I hadn't originated the conversation, the fact remained that I was now talking to the woman I had wanted to talk to for several months. My response, rather more pedestrian than hers—"I'll get some coffee"—was sufficient to start a relationship that, fifty-four years later, is still going strong. And I still provide the coffee in the morning.

Step-fathering

I can't remember the exact nature of our conversation when I returned to the table with our coffees that Friday morning in late April, but it certainly was nothing more than pleasant trivialities. Two people, clearly attracted to each other, trying to share some basic information appropriate for the start of a relationship. And, of course, to be as funny and charming as possible to guarantee that the other's interest didn't flag. After an indecently short time, I knew I wanted to see Judith again and invited her out to dinner for that evening. She later claimed she was quite sure her answer would end things before they began. "I would like to," she said, "but I have two children who are home with me this weekend, so I can't." "Let's see how fast he gets out of here," she thought, "now that he's heard about the children." My response completely surprised her: "How about Monday?"

Judith's skepticism about the odds of my hanging around after learning that she wasn't free and untethered was perfectly understandable. Who would deliberately choose an instant family of three when the city was awash with unencumbered women actively seeking single men? She was unquestionably right that conventional wisdom wouldn't have predicted a dinner invitation for Monday night once I was informed about why she couldn't make Friday.

But conventional wisdom couldn't account for two quite disparate factors that produced my suggestion for a Monday night meeting. The first was the strength of my attraction. After months of fantasizing, I just needed to see more of her. I was not about to let her disappear. The second, perhaps less easy to understand, had to do with the fact that I found something positively appealing in the notion of going out with a woman with children. Rather than dissuading me, this information engendered the feeling that it was a way of being catapulted into real life. Most of my friends were by this point married (I was thirty-two at the time) and starting families, while I had the distinct sense that I had become temporarily stalled, looking in at life from the outside. As my relationship with Judith flourished, the thought of taking on her two boys seemed less like a burden and more like an enhancement of my existence. I, too, could experience the full human complexity I was seeking.

Picnics in the park, wrestling matches, teaching them poker—all of these struck me as things that men should be doing, in addition to grown-up career pursuits, and I took delight in being involved in them. But, of course, I was only going out with their mother; I wasn't living with them, providing part of the world of adult discipline, intruding on their home space, having them intrude on mine. I was no kind of a father, step- or otherwise. Besides, they had a perfectly functional father living a few minutes away who took care of paternal duties. So I can't say I knew what I was getting into, other than the fact that life seemed fuller and more interesting than when I was living alone. More complicated, to be sure, but also more fun. I liked my connection with Erik and Stephen. As my presence with the boys and Judith became an increasingly commonplace feature of their household, the conversation heated up a bit. "Are you going to marry my mommy?" I was asked one evening while I was saying good night. If I can remember the question, I don't remember the answer I generated, although I am certain I avoided giving anything away. Marriage remained a scary proposition, but marrying a woman with two children didn't strike me as any scarier. Perhaps it should have. Of course, since I didn't know myself, my lack of a serious response made perfect sense.

As the summer of 1970 approached and plans had to be made for where we would all be, Judith and I decided it was time. Wherever we were, we should be together. And lest we be seen skulking around, trying to avoid the charge of corrupting the moral nature of innocent children by living in sin, this more or less meant getting married. That would not be a problem. The problem was what to do afterward with our new family structure.

But first the marriage, the day my father later confided to my sister was the worst of his life. While I didn't understand that feature of this happy occasion, I did recognize the day's dreadful heat. The boys wandered around like lost souls, surrounded by perspiring adults they didn't know who expressed little interest in them. I can't imagine how unpleasant they must have found the entire experience.

If I had any question about their feelings, it was answered rather tersely the next evening. We had spent our wedding night at a hotel, with Judy's parents taking care of the boys at her—now our—apartment. We returned the following day to our first dinner together as our newly fabricated family. Things were cheery as we ate, and we finally came to what clearly was the meal's treat: a slice of delicious wedding cake for dessert. "Would you like a piece?" Judy asked the boys, obviously knowing what the answer had to be. "No," Erik blurted out. "I hated the wedding . . . I . . . I mean the wedding cake."

STEP-FATHERING

Launched by my father's paternal blessing and Erik's rejection of the cake, I was certainly off and running in my new life.

But where exactly? Fortunately, an answer was immediately at hand. Columbia offered a summer program, funded by the Ford Foundation, for incoming students with somewhat sketchy academic backgrounds who wanted to satisfy the college's English composition requirement before school actually began. Perhaps not surprisingly, many of them were football players. The engineering school owned a large property in Connecticut, known as Camp Columbia, where the football team used to go for preseason practice. As the name suggested, it was not unlike a summer camp, with dormitories, a dining hall and kitchen staffed by cooks skilled in the arts of preparing red meat for growing football players, a basketball court, a rec hall, and access to a lake. Perfect in every way. I had been asked if I were interested in teaching there before the change in my marital status and had said yes. Now all I had to do was inform the director that my housing needs had expanded. The single room I had planned to occupy would no longer be sufficient for my new family.

"Oh, dear," he answered, when I revealed this to him over the phone. "I am afraid the larger houses have all been taken. There is no place where you can stay."

This was entirely unexpected. What could we do? Judith wondered if there was a motel nearby that could house us, but in addition to being inconvenient, it would devour the small amount of money I was being paid for my pedagogical services. No solution there. It looked as if the perfect arrangement for the summer was not perfect after all.

Several days after learning there was no room at the inn, I got a surprise call from the property's manager. "Dr. Rosenthal," he said. "I have good news. I had forgotten that there is a large farmhouse on the grounds that is available for you and your family." This information, delightful as it was, struck me as odd. How do you manage to forget the existence of a capacious farmhouse when you are struggling to find a place to house an instructor who otherwise might not be able to participate in a program in which he is needed? A few seconds later, I got my clarification: "But there is a slight problem that I wanted to share with you before you agree to stay there."

"Sure," I replied. "What is it?"

"The caretaker who was the previous occupant committed suicide by blowing his brains out in the living room."

While I certainly wasn't prepared for that as the explanation, I can't say it bothered me. But I recognized that my newly minted wife might have a different view, and so I said I would speak to her and then get back to him.

I was correct: not only did she have a different view, she said she would under no circumstances live in a place where a suicide had occurred. I tried to point out that the house was exactly right for the four of us, that there were no better alternatives, that the whole summer depended on our taking it. I prevailed; she agreed—with one stipulation. She would stay there as long as I promised that we would never go into the room where the caretaker had allegedly shot himself.

As that room—the living room—was the heart of the house, with a large fireplace and a comfortable couch, it was difficult to agree never to enter it, but since those were the terms, I had to capitulate. "OK," I said, firmly believing this was a crazy condition, "we will avoid the room of death altogether."

Which we did for three or four days. No lovely fires, no family frolics, until Judy, coming finally to appreciate that this was not a reasonable arrangement, withdrew her veto and allowed us all to enjoy the comforts of the house's large central room. She even suspended her insistence that the stain on the windowsill was old brain matter from the suicide and endorsed the more sensible hypothesis that it came from the plant that had been watered there for years.

Her acceptance of the previously forbidden space did not come without a cost. The very first night after we had played in front of the fireplace, Judith woke up screaming in my ear, yelling for help to rescue her from a dreadful dream. Fifty years of happy marriage later, I am still called upon to save her in the middle of a sound sleep from some awful impending disaster. There is no doubt that the lifelong assault of terror that occasionally overwhelms Judith at night owes itself to her initial willingness to enter the room she desperately wanted to avoid.

• • • •

Camp Columbia was a happy time for the new Rosenthal family. Besides a few hours each day of teaching and tutoring, the rest was uncomplicated pleasure. My nonexistent skills of fathering or step-fathering were not called upon, as the major decision-making in any given day concerned which combination of the available entertainments—family jigsaws, swimming, touch football, basketball, endless board and card games—should occupy us. At the end of the summer the boys went off horseback riding with their father while Judith and I flew to Yugoslavia on our official honeymoon.

Returning to our 139th Street apartment, which I bought from Gerry, Judith's ex-husband, I commenced understanding what fathers did. I had no idea, so it was a steep learning curve. Coming into the apartment from being outside with the boys, for example, I had to realize that flopping down to read something was no longer an option. Organizing baths for two dirty boys was. Chores that had never occurred to me of a helping, supervisory, interactive sort now began to become second nature. Life with two children, I came rapidly to appreciate, bore little resemblance to what I had experienced in my previous bachelorhood. But it was, after all, what I had opted for. I just had to figure it out.

And figure it out I did. The pleasure I took in my relationship with Erik and Stephen, at least from my perspective, was never a problem. I enjoyed them and very much felt they contributed to my happiness. I always felt I contributed to theirs as well. Judith was anxious lest tensions develop between us, her first impulse being to intervene to try to ensure smooth functioning. I argued that I needed to form my own ties with them, independent of hers, including whatever difficulties might have to be solved. If it was to succeed, the three of us, not the four, would have to work at it.

One major tactical challenge I faced was how to be a loving and supportive presence—a father figure, in other words—without casting myself as a rival with the boys' actual father. When one of them asked early on whether he should sign his name on his schoolwork "Rosenthal" or "Gaull," I knew I had to tread carefully so as not to complicate what had at the very least to be confusing for them. I did my best to make sure they didn't think I was trying to replace their father.

It wasn't always easy. Sometime in late December 1970, the year we were married, Erik was playing on the floor in my office. Sonny Liston, the boxer, had just died, and Erik was in a kind of absent-minded way lamenting his death. "Well," I said, "of course it is sad when anyone dies, particularly someone young, but Liston was certainly not a distinguished human being, and I am not sure he is worth all of your mourning."

"I know," he responded, "but there are so many others I would rather have died."

Sensing that I might be on the verge of some interesting emotional material, I gently prodded. "Like whom?" I asked.

STEP-FATHERING

I forget the first name he mentioned. The second, for some reason, has remained with me for these past fifty years: "And you, for another."

I can't say I wasn't surprised, though I actually thought it represented a healthy way of admitting to painful feelings that had to be gnawing at him. I might in fact have been a loving stepfather who taught him poker, but at the same time it could hardly be denied that in some fundamental way I didn't really belong there. So while I was delicately trying to maintain the proper balance between connected stepfather and noncompetitive father, the boys were clearly wrestling in different ways with more primitive feelings. As I knew of no handbooks to consult on how to navigate these situations, I could only trust the wisdom of my instincts, giving the boys the space they needed to adjust to an arrangement for which they had never exactly volunteered.

I think it is fair to say it all worked out. If it wasn't the family they initially knew, it was a family in which we grew to love one another. Judith and I did our best to ensure that their full life with us was never at the expense of nurturing times with their father. I am confident we succeeded in that. I confess that I was concerned that the introduction of another intrusive presence into their existences—in this case our son Noah in 1972—might pose difficulties for them, but it didn't. On the contrary, they saw the arrival of a baby brother as an interesting new feature of life that did not interfere with their pleasures. More of another toy than any kind of burden. The greatest challenge posed by Noah, in fact, was to get him to understand what "Dad" meant, since he only overheard the boys refer to Gerry, not me, as "Dad." "Why don't we use Dad's car?" he would helpfully suggest when we might be planning a trip. Eventually he accepted me as his father, without the prompting of his half brothers.

Board Member

My young friend Randy, son of multimillionaire real estate tycoon Al Lerner, said he couldn't tell me what exactly was happening but that something was taking place that might result in some extra money for me. He estimated the probability at about twenty-five percent. He would keep me informed. Over the next weeks the percentage rose steadily: forty, sixty, seventy-five. I still had no idea of what might be occurring, though it was beginning to look as if whatever it was would in fact occur. Finally the decisive phone call from Randy: "OK, it's done, we are going to have dinner tomorrow night at the Carlyle Hotel with my dad. He'll explain. He has just completed taking a credit card company public on the New York Stock Exchange and he has put you on the board. Please be totally surprised; I had sworn not to tell you anything."

I had gotten to know Al, an active and wonderfully generous Columbia alumnus, since joining the Office of the Dean in 1972. We had become good friends, and when Randy arrived as a Columbia undergraduate in the fall of 1980, it was inevitable that I turned into his mentor. By the time the three of us went to dinner twelve years later, that mentorship had developed into a close friendship. When he got married, I gave the congratulatory toast, as Al felt awkward about speaking in public.

At the restaurant I couldn't tell whether Al knew that I knew. He was pretty shrewd about everything and might well have sensed that the amazement I expressed was slightly canned, but he never let on. Over the extremely expensive smoked salmon, he filled in the details of what Randy had pledged to keep from me: how he had become a large investor in MNC, a financial holding company, which owned, among other things, a small but promising credit card unit. With MNC struggling, Al thought to try to interest various large corporations in purchasing its MBNA credit card. Because of MNC's difficulties, however, no one wanted to pay what Al considered a fair price for it, counting on the fact that the company's problems would force it, sooner rather than later, to accept a meager offer. This was not the sort of tactic designed to please him, and he decided to undercut the buyers waiting for a bargain by taking the company public. Several years' work and an immense amount of his own money brought Al to the point where MBNA was about to open on the New York Stock Exchange. All that was left for him to provide were the names of his board of directors.

While everybody expected the standard big names—the Vernon Jordans, the Christine Todd Whitmans, and the like—Al was having none of that. No iconic star directors for him. As he narrated the story to me over dinner, everything was in place except for the identities of his board. Wall Street and potential investors were eager to discover whom Al had chosen. Finally he agreed to announce it. His first name was Jim Berick's. Who is Jim Berick? people wanted to know. "Berick is a Columbia fraternity brother and my lawyer," Al responded, "and I wouldn't think of having a board without him." Who else? "Stuart Markowitz," said Al. Who is he? they asked "He is my personal physician," Al stated, "and since we'll be doing a lot of business with hospitals and doctors, it's important that he be there."

Clearly Al was hugely enjoying both defying people's expectations and letting me know the pleasure he took in it. But the most outrageous moment was yet to come. Eyeballs were no doubt already rolling around in countless heads when Al revealed the name of the next director, someone, it is fair to say, little known to the cognoscenti of corporate boards: Michael Rosenthal. "He is a dean at Columbia," Al deliciously explained, "and he needs the money." Al then released the names of the other two directors, said he didn't want to discuss the matter any further and that if there were those unhappy with his selections, they were free to take their investments and leave. None did. Given the extraordinary growth of the company, which went on to become the largest independent credit card issuer in the world, it was a decision no one ever regretted.

So now I was a fully certified corporate director, or at least I would be as soon as I purchased the $1,000 worth of MBNA stock required of all directors. I lacked only one other thing: even the vaguest knowledge of what my duties might be. After finishing his description of the origins and development of MBNA, Al addressed this problem directly. "Do you have any idea what you will be doing?" he bluntly asked me.

"Well," I stammered, "I guess the board makes decisions about the direction of the company, business strategies, stuff like that."

Al looked closely at me, mild incredulity coming over his face. "Michael, I have put one hundred million of my own dollars into this company; do you think I am interested in having you, as great an English professor and dean as you are, tell me what to do with it?"

Good point, I thought. Hard to refute. "OK," I said, "let me give it another try. I think my job as director is to support the wisdom of the chairman's decisions and to ensure that the company does what the chairman decides is best for it."

Al broke into a smile of satisfaction. "Excellent—I couldn't have put it better myself."

Having exhibited such a sophisticated understanding of the role of the MBNA board, I was soon launched into an exotic, ten-year adventure of corporate governance normally not available to literature scholars and deans who wrote books about Virginia Woolf. Four or five times a year I would be helicoptered down from New York's West Side heliport to Newark, Delaware, where the company's headquarters were located. (MBNA was particularly proud of its helicopter fleet, I should add, emphasizing that with two pilots and two sets of controls on every machine, it was not possible to travel more safely. Certainly my trips to and from the city were flawless, and it wasn't until after I had left the board that the helicopter that ordinarily carried me to my meeting crashed into the Hudson River, shortly after takeoff, with six executives on it. Fortunately, no one was seriously injured, though I experienced a good bit of vicariously retrospective anxiety imagining what might have happened had I been under the water working to escape from my seat belt.)

Sitting around gigantic, elegant conference tables with senior management, listening to reports and scrutinizing graphs charting the prodigious profitability of the company, I worked hard at developing my financial literacy (though I am certain I never fooled anybody) and conducting myself in an appropriately businesslike manner. I wore my double-breasted suits to meetings, smoked cigars when they were handed out, asked what I thought were timely questions, nodded sagely in endorsing good performances, and, needless to say, voted as expected. I even succeeded in getting into trouble on one occasion, when I expressed concern for some behavior I thought seriously problematic, driving the choleric president of the company (not Al) into a rage. I didn't quite realize how bad my offense was until the next meeting, when he distributed a reallocation proposal of directorial responsibilities in which I was dropped from the influential finance committee. I could hardly speak on my own behalf, and I knew that Berick and Markowitz would not challenge a plan from President Charlie Cawley, so my survival on the committee depended on the response of the lead director, Ben Civiletti, who had been Jimmy Carter's attorney general. A real director, in short, not one of Al's friendly amateurs.

When Ben began speaking of his view of the situation, I listened as closely as possible to try to detect where his argument was heading, but I confess I had absolutely no idea whether he was for or against me. He demonstrated the verbal skills of an experienced statesman, supporting, criticizing, and covering all points in between. By the end of his comments he had placated Charlie, gently chided me, and succeeded in keeping me on the committee. I was both grateful and admiring.

Functioning simultaneously as dean and board member involved me in two entirely different galaxies. While Columbia famously limped along in a kind of haphazard administrative way, skimping here, cutting budgets there, Charlie insisted that everything at MBNA be meticulously organized, exquisitely finished. Expense was not only not an issue, it should never even be thought about, no less mentioned. When some of us expressed concern about the cost of air travel for executives flying to meetings on MBNA's private fleet of planes, Charlie could almost not speak: "You mean you would want our people to go on scheduled commercial airlines?" Absolutely not an option.

When we started to issue credit cards in Britain in 1993 we flew to Chester, in the north of England, where the company would be located. We arrived at night, and after breakfast the next morning we all assembled outside the hotel for our trip to the new offices. We noticed large crowds congregating on both sides of the street, staring at the procession of Daimlers pulling up in front of the hotel. We wondered whom they were looking for, speculating that royalty might be around, maybe even the queen. But no, we were the object of their gawking, the string of Daimlers Charlie had hired to take us to the bank elevating our importance in the eyes of the Chester citizens. Such is the power of a handsome Daimler, which Charlie well knew.

My brilliant career as a director lasted ten years. It came to an abrupt halt in 2002 when Al died of brain cancer. Not that I had to leave because of his death; the issue arose because of what followed. Al had always intended Randy to succeed him as chairman of the board, and after his death we held a directors' meeting to vote him in. A perfunctory discussion preceded a unanimous vote. No problem there. Randy was now the next chairman of the board. The only question: What would his salary be in his new position?

Charlie Cawley, eager to stay on close terms with the Lerner family, opened the conversation with a recommendation that shocked me: $2 million. I didn't see how Randy, as a relatively young man (forty-two) with no experience in running the company, could possibly merit such a sum. Remember, it was 2002. With all that I didn't know as a director, one thing I did know—and actually took seriously—was my obligation to try to protect the interests of the stockholders and the health of the company. How could such inflated compensation serve anybody's interest besides Randy's? In addition, I couldn't entirely rid myself of the notion that with the enormous expansion of Al's fortune during the ten years' growth of MBNA, Randy, his mother, and his sister were now all legitimate billionaires. Should we really worry that we might be underpaying him?

The number $500,000 surfaced in the discussion, and that seemed a more appropriate sum to me. Not up to Charlie's suggestion, perhaps, but not exactly piker's pay, either. As we went back and forth, I began to realize that I was in a more complicated predicament than I had originally understood. As one of Al's homegrown directors whose life had been materially changed by serving on the board, was I prepared to vote against what I knew Al would want, not to speak of Randy and his mother, in order to honor what I thought was right? And what about the consequences that would surely follow if I failed to support the family? Rosenthal self-interest decreed that I back Charlie's figure, so why was I having such trouble?

Finally the time came to declare where the five of us stood. Jim and Stuart, Al's lawyer and doctor, felt no conflict, as I'd known they wouldn't. Lerner loyalty was their highest calling, as it was assumed to be mine. Their decision was not difficult in the least. The other two directors, Ben Civiletti and Bill Jews, occupied a more independent space that enabled them to vote their own uncompromised judgment. They resisted Charlie's $2 million suggestion. That left me. I knew what was expected of me, that these are the compromises that mature people make in a complex life that is never as pure as you would like it to be, but try as I might, I couldn't bring myself to do it. I voted against Charlie's number.

That turned out to be my last official action as a board member. The next day Ben, as the lead director, called me to say that with all the recent public scrutiny about the qualifications and pay scales of directors of corporate boards, it was felt best for the company that I step down. Not his idea, I understood, but I realized that he, too, was not impervious to Lerner family pressures. Ten years of service on the board aside, in denying Randy his salary I had proved unworthy of continued board membership, and Ben had been instructed to deliver the sentence. I asked if Stuart, whose credentials were no better than mine, was also leaving; Ben, a master at the art of how not to answer, didn't. Later that day Randy called to say that he'd been disappointed to learn that I apparently lacked faith in his abilities. I said I would be happy to explain why I'd voted the way I had, but he claimed he had to go and we never spoke again.

My Table at Rao's

I never knew Mimi Sheraton, the *New York Times* food critic during the late 1970s, but she profoundly influenced the entire Rosenthal family as no other journalist ever did.

It was August 1977, and Judy had just read her review of Rao's, a tiny (eight-table) southern Italian restaurant located in East Harlem since 1896, to which she had given three stars. Judy was smitten: the size, its authenticity, the unpretentiousness, the simple but delicious ingredients. Exactly her kind of place. We had to eat there immediately. Easier said than done. I called and called and called. Most of the time the phone was busy. When it wasn't busy, there were no tables. And keep in mind, the place was not open on the weekends. Or for lunch. Maybe next month or the month after. Also maybe never. At last, sometime in the fall, my perseverance paid off and I secured a reservation. Forty-seven years later we are still eating there. My table awaits me the second Friday of every month. I call only when we can't come, which is not often.

Of course, in 1977 we didn't know about tables at Rao's. All we knew was that we were thrilled finally to have gotten into the restaurant we most wanted to eat at in New York. While food is the proper business of restaurants, the culinary pleasures of Rao's accounted for only part of its total experience. To walk down the four steps into the dark, tin-roofed restaurant was to enter a crowded, noisy, intense universe of pulsating energy and year-round tacky Christmas decorations; of a wonderful old jukebox into which you would inject dollar bills, thereby producing the sounds of Frank Sinatra and the Ink Spots; of Jocko, the fat black dog who roamed from table to table, growing ever fatter as customers slipped him food; of Nicky the Vest, the bartender who owned one hundred and fifty or so vests and sported an enormous ring signifying his belonging to the Bartender Hall of Fame; of fabulous neighborhood characters like Frankie Nose and Johnnie Roast Beef.

The muse of the place, who presided over the eight tables, making everybody feel privileged and wanted, was Frank Pellegrino—otherwise known as "Frankie No" for being the person to convey the unhappy reality to those seeking a reservation about why they couldn't have one. A man of consummate grace and charm, Frank, at least when we first came, prepared the appetizers, sat down at every table to explain the food options (there are no menus at Rao's), led the restaurant in the almost nightly singing of "My Girl" (he had worked as a singer until he was undone by a paralyzed vocal cord), and, if you were lucky, would join your table at the end of the evening to discuss politics. Frank took his politics seriously and was a passionate Democrat. Judy asked him one evening how many clients he had ever convinced to share his views and he said, "None."

In addition to running the restaurant, Frank was an actor, a literary agent, and an entrepreneur who turned Rao's pasta and pasta sauces into nationally distributed products available in supermarkets across the country. On a decidedly more personal note, he was surely the only restaurateur in America who read my book on the British Boy

Scout movement. He also knew precisely how to cultivate and protect the unique spirit that was Rao's. The one time my wife wondered if he could do something about the noise level, Frank gently responded, "Judy, it's not a library."

According to Frank's own testimony, as a neighborhood kid he'd always hoped that someday, when he grew up, he'd work at the restaurant owned by his aunt Anna and her husband, Vincent Rao. When Anna asked him to come and help out for a couple of weeks in 1972, he had no idea what that simple request would make of his life—or of the little-known restaurant on East 114th Street he would develop into a hugely successful business.

In 1977 Anna and Vincent did the cooking in the small, open kitchen facing the entrance, Vincent, tall, wearing his signature brown leather Stetson hat; Anna, petite, elegantly coifed, with tinted glasses, cigarette precariously perched on the back of the Viking stove, impossibly impeccable in her white turtleneck sweater, which remained mysteriously unsullied by the chops and sauces cooking away around her. It was as if they didn't dare besmirch her.

We loved everything about the restaurant from the beginning—the food, the people, the ambience, even the guests who crowded the bar—and did our best to find a way back whenever we could. Getting to know Frank helped, though it was no guarantee, and after several years Judy managed to start up a friendship of sorts with Anna, talking to her at the bar at the end of the evening, after she had stopped cooking and as we were about to leave.

Judy was curious about how everything tasted so good and kept on pressing Frank for what the secrets were. He insisted there were no secrets, just good ingredients, well prepared. Judy remained skeptical, claiming there had to be tricks that Anna had developed over the years. She continued to badger Frank, until she finally put to him what I thought was a bizarre request: Did he think that Anna might permit her to spend some time in the kitchen watching what she did? Frank gulped, said his aunt had never allowed any such arrangement, but that he would ask. When he next came out of the kitchen, he seemed totally surprised. "Anna agreed," he told a startled Judy. "You have to bring a pile of notecards and write down everything she says and does. And come in the middle of the afternoon to watch how Annie Maguire, who does the prep work, sets things up. Above all, no perfume. My aunt hates perfume," Frank emphasized.

And so began Judy's extraordinary week as an intern in Anna Rao's kitchen. She would arrive around three-thirty with her three-by-fives in time to see Annie receive and scrutinize the vegetables (and on one occasion return a box as unsatisfactory), chop the garlic, ready the fish salad, prepare the peppers, and carry out the myriad other tasks that had to be accomplished if Vincent and Anna were to perform their magic in the evening. The detailed recipes and cooking instructions on the notecards suggest how conscientiously Judy followed Anna around the kitchen, listening to her every word. Not only did she learn the techniques of producing the sumptuous veal chops with vinegar peppers and the exquisite lemon chicken, but at the end of the evening she was included with the family as they ate their dinner. After a week of intensive study and delicious eating, she came to acknowledge Frank's position that there were no secrets, just marvelous cooking.

One of the happy consequences of Judy's Rao's interlude was her closer relationship with Anna. Judy loved Anna's stories of the Italian neighborhood, once the largest in New York, and the role Vincent played as the prominent, generous "don" who would help people in need, regardless of what time of the day or night they came by the house, located right next to Rao's. Judy would bring coffee cake by on Saturdays, when Rao's was closed, and ply Anna with questions about what New York's first "Little Italy" was like. It was at one of these visits that Judy learned that what Anna most wanted to do was hear Pavarotti at the opera. "I'll get the tickets," Judy declared. "And I'll get the car," Anna replied. Judy discovered a Saturday performance of *Rigoletto*, Anna procured a limousine, and off they went to fulfill Anna's fondest dream.

Their burgeoning friendship still didn't make it any easier to eat at Rao's. We didn't know at the time about the possibility of being allocated a table, and so we would scramble in an ad hoc fashion each time we went to try to arrange the next reservation, some months in the future. Finally Judy raised a question that struck me as absurd as asking whether Anna would allow her to observe what went on in the kitchen. Since we had begun to learn about "regulars" who were granted a monthly slot, Judy mused, perhaps Frank would be willing to include us in that group.

With all the pressures on Frank, and with our decided non-celebrity status, that seemed extremely unlikely to me, and I urged her not to embarrass us by requiring him to turn us down. Judy doesn't embarrass easily, however, and the next time we were having our end-of-the-evening chat with Frank, she posed the question: We love eating here, she said, but we struggle to make reservations. Did he think we could get a standing table? Instead of the delicately offered rejection I expected, Frank got up and said he would consult the books. He came back a few minutes later. "How would the last Friday (later changed to the second Friday) in every month do?" he inquired.

Done. As simple as all that, without having to appeal to the better angels of Frank's nature, we had been effortlessly inducted into the fellowship of Rao's. We no longer had to negotiate about a date in the far distant future on which we could be accommodated: our

MY TABLE AT RAO'S

booth for four would always be available for us. The only stipulation required that we notify Rao's in time for them to fill the table if we were not able to keep the reservation.

My first effort to cancel proved more difficult than one would think. I began calling several days in advance, eager to demonstrate my reliability. But the secret of Rao's was that the phone was never picked up: of course no one answered. One day passed, than two. By Wednesday I'd panicked, fearing that I would be charged with the heinous crime of indifference and my special status revoked. So I did what arguably no customer at a restaurant had ever done before: I took a cab to tell them I wouldn't be there on Friday. They were amazed and, I think, a bit horrified that I had gone to the trouble of getting a taxi, and shared with me the simpler technique for cancellation obviously known to all the regulars but me: the cell-phone number carried by one of the waitstaff. It certainly made things easier; I never had to panic again.

Our more than forty years of connection to Rao's produced joyous, festive evenings that have composed a special part of our New York existence: sumptuous meals, rich memories. Included in both was my one Friday date that happened to fall on Christmas Eve. I arrived, dimly aware of the Italian-American tradition of serving seafood at that dinner—the so-called Feast of the Seven Fishes—but never imagining that Frank planned to honor the celebration by delivering seven different courses of seafood, from lobsters to scampi to baked clams, at no cost, to those of us lucky to be eating there that evening. And while I could graciously accept Frank's lovely generosity in feeding us without charge, I could see no reason why we couldn't at least pay for our drinks. But when I tried to do that, I was told that at Rao's Christmas Eve was entirely on the house, no exceptions. A memorable instance of pure Frank.

SCRAPS, ORTS, AND FRAGMENTS

In late December 2003, my table missed by four days a Rao's evening that Frank certainly did not appreciate. Louie "Lump Lump" Barone, a small-time thug with a rather large belly (hence the two lumps), was standing at the bar when an aspiring Broadway actress who was a guest at a table began, under Frank's encouragement, to sing. A customer next to Barone did not approve of her voice and suggested she stop. Barone urged him to be quiet, a suggestion the man found offensive. As Barone later testified, "He insulted me, so I had to do something about it." His solution was to pull out his .38 and shoot him in the chest, then watch as the man lurched away from the bar and died in front of the kitchen.

Having clearly seen his share of gangster movies, Barone knew exactly what to do next. He calmly put down his gun and walked out of the restaurant, unfortunately encountering two uniformed policemen sitting in their parked car, to whom he explained that a shooting had just taken place. An off-duty detective who was having dinner then came running out, supplying the detail Barone had overlooked: that he was, in fact, the shooter. After the full panoply of police arrived, the officer in charge instructed everybody to come down to the precinct to answer questions. Frank interrupted: "These are my guests. They're not going anywhere." They didn't. Barone, who later died in prison, apologized to Frank for causing such trouble.

Vincent died in 1994. Anna, who was ill at the time, said she wanted to stay alive long enough to ensure that Vincent received a proper burial. She did, and died several weeks later. Frank died in 2017. With the absence of the Raos and Frank, the restaurant couldn't possibly be the same, and it's not. The food is still great, it's still impossible to get a reservation, the place still seems to exude more family warmth than anything else, but it misses the beating heart of Frank, which remained always discernible above the din.

MY TABLE AT RAO'S

In the obituary she wrote, Mimi Sheraton called him "raffish and authentic," which comes pretty close to some of his essential truths. What her description omits, among many qualities, were his empathy and loyalty as a friend. A number of years ago, Frank was willing to renounce his principles in order to rescue me from a difficult situation involving Rao's into which I had foolishly stumbled.

I was at the time, a member of Al Lerner's corporate board of MBNA. There are very few favors that ordinary people can do for billionaires, so when Al let it be known that he was eager to eat sausages and peppers at Rao's, I said I would be happy to take him. I knew that he had several high-profile friends—Ace Greenberg of Bear Stearns, Senator Alfonse D'Amato—who had tables there, and he wanted to see what it was all about. I was too naïve to realize that he was less interested in savoring the sausages than in gaining the same privileges that his pals had—a regular table at Rao's—and that I was to be the instrument of that opportunity.

When Frank sat down at our booth at the end of the evening to chat, I was horrified to hear Al commit the unconscionable: he told Frank that he would like the capacity to make a reservation whenever he wanted. A moment of huge awkwardness, with only one possible resolution: Frank summoning all the charm and tact at his disposal to say no.

Al was clearly outraged. I suspect that billionaires don't get told "no" often, particularly when it comes to a request to eat at a decidedly unfancy neighborhood restaurant. But "Frankie No" hadn't earned his name by saying yes, and he was not the sort to be impressed by Al's wealth. He was experienced in rejecting all manner of the rich and powerful.

The ride home in Al's limo was not pleasant. Al was fuming, and Norma, his wife, was incensed that her husband could have been dismissed in that way. After we were dropped off, Judy insisted that

SCRAPS, ORTS, AND FRAGMENTS

this was a big-time mess that would have to be addressed; I maintained the position that Al was an adult and if he couldn't make a reservation at Rao's, it couldn't possibly be something that would genuinely upset him. Judy said I didn't appreciate how angry this had made him; she would call Norma the next day to determine how the Lerners were feeling.

Judy, it turned out, was right. Norma explained just how furious Al was, adding that he couldn't understand how I could continue to go to a restaurant that had treated him so badly. The message couldn't have been delivered more clearly: if I wanted to remain an MBNA board member, I would have to display my allegiance to Al by forgetting about Rao's.

As I didn't want to give up either connection, I concocted what I thought a clever solution and used the phone number Frank had given me sometime before to call him at home. I told him I felt I had been set up and apologized for putting him in an embarrassing situation. He said it was not a problem and asked what he could do to make things better. I revealed my plan: give Al my dates and I would manage to find my own irregular ways to get there.

Frank, who understood how the board membership had contributed to my life, replied that such an arrangement would not be acceptable to him. If I wanted Al to be able to book a table from time to time, he was agreeable to that plan, but he would not permit me to renounce my Fridays. Did I want him to call Al? he asked. As long as I could assure Al that he could get to Rao's, I could handle it, I said. Frank need not do anything more. He had already done more than enough. He confirmed that I could in full confidence let Al know that Rao's was open to him.

I called Al and passed on the new information. He was delighted but cautious. "You mean," he said, making sure there would be no room for misunderstanding, "if I have my girl call Rao's and arrange a date, a table will be available for me?" (I had foolishly failed to appreciate that billionaires tend not to make their own reservations.) "Exactly," I said emphatically. One phone call restored me to his good graces. Al had access to his peppers, and I stayed on the board. "Frankie Yes" had gone well out of his way for me, and I will never forget his willingness to help.

Seasonal Effervescence

For a woman who loved travel, both real and vicarious, and found maps endlessly fascinating, it had to be the perfect job. From the mid-seventies to the mid-eighties, Judith ran a British travel office, located on Seventy-ninth Street off Madison Avenue, that served American travel agents planning trips in England and Scotland for their affluent American clients. The small, posh company for which she worked, based in London and called Take-A-Guide, featured charming, certified Blue Badge driver-guides who, for astronomical sums, would meet their customers at the airport in private cars and tour them around on itineraries worked out by Judith in conjunction with the agents. Accommodations were in varieties of châteaux and superb country house hotels, elegance and expense the necessary requirements for guest satisfaction. What I understand today are known as "destination experts," highly trained professionals skilled at devising the most stimulating journeys to the most interesting places in the United Kingdom, were in the primitive seventies and eighties simply Judith, poring over her maps and road atlas to put together the consummate travel experience.

The American agents who came to rely heavily on Judith's expertise were often lamentably uninformed about the country to which they were sending their clientele. The outstanding instance of this was the man who wanted to arrange a car trip from London to Edinburgh as soon as the customer's plane arrived in London. "No good," Judith replied, "too far." The agent persisted. Judith thought she could help him see the problem by getting him to look at a map. He followed her suggestion and came back to the phone. "I see Edinburg" (as he pronounced it), "but I don't see any Edinboro." Judith also liked the account of one of the company's driver-guides who reported that two women who were being driven around England's southern coast asked him when they might have a chance to see the British isles.

Besides immersing Judith in the travel world she enjoyed and providing her with memorable instances of incompetence and ignorance, Take-A-Guide afforded her other material benefits as well. Because she was the sole occupant of the town house office, she could take our dog with her without fear of disturbing anyone. And when Noah was on vacation from school, there was no need to devise complicated plans to look after him. He simply packed up some books and accompanied her to work.

But there was another feature of the job that delighted Judith. Supplying the agents who contacted her with suggestions of extraordinary places for their clients to stay invariably put her in contact with the owners and general managers of these high-end properties. While making clear to them that the room reservations originated from Take-A-Guide, she let it be known that the more personally familiar she was with the particular comforts they offered their guests, the more persuasive her recommendations could be. So if during the off-season there were some rooms remaining empty, she would be happy to come over and look around. This, in the travel trade, is known as a familiarization trip, or, more colloquially, a "fam trip." The virtues of appealing to those who were responsible for sending the clients were not lost on the proprietors, and it didn't take long before Judith and I were studying the calendar to see when we could accept the lovely invitations for their hospitality. Including her husband and young son was certainly not a problem, either.

No one had problems accommodating us, with one exception. Oddly enough—or perhaps not—the sole owner who said his hotel was fully booked was an American. As we had already agreed to eat supper there with friends, we found a pub not too far away that had some vacant rooms, told Noah he could watch television until we came back, and drove off for dinner. Midway to the hotel we were engulfed by an enormous, unexpected blizzard, making it almost impossible to see. I actually walked ahead of the car to ensure that it stayed on the road. We had no choice but to continue, there being no way, in our pre-cell-phone world, to consult with our friends, who had driven up from Exeter, about what to do.

The four of us finally succeeded in getting to the hotel, where we had a sumptuous meal, worthy of all the praise Judith had heard about the Michelin-starred restaurant. Meanwhile the storm showed no sign of letting up, and going out into the blinding snow seemed a foolish and dangerous option. There appeared to be no solution, until the maître d' suddenly appeared at our table in the dining room with an entirely unexpected one: the owner, he explained, was concerned about our safety and would like to offer us complimentary rooms to stay the night. So having assured Judith months earlier that nothing was available at the inn, he had managed, under the duress of a fierce snow deluge, to discover space for two families. We immediately called Noah, negotiated a ten-pound bribe for him to spend the night without us, and enjoyed a pleasant sleep before returning to the pub early the next morning. We even received free toothbrushes and toothpaste.

SEASONAL EFFERVESCENCE

During Judith's tenure at Take-A-Guide we must have taken a half dozen fam trips. All were splendid, only one bringing with it any stressful moments. Owned over the course of four or five centuries by assorted earls and barons, Eastwell Manor, in Kent, finally emerged in the twentieth century as a glorious country house hotel. We were thrilled to be able to spend time there and have dinner in the very elegant restaurant. I had always understood that fam trips were on the house, as it would make little sense to charge people whose favorable review you were trying to solicit. This applied to the dinner as well. What I was never quite certain about was the status of the wine, as I could honestly see no reason why I shouldn't be responsible for the cost. If the hotel wanted to include that in the complimentary nature of the whole experience, fine, but otherwise I would have no problem paying for it. In fact I never did, but I wouldn't have objected if asked. I always proceeded as if I might.

On this particular evening I ordered a modestly priced burgundy to accompany what I knew would be our distinguished meal. Judith and I raised our glasses to toast each other and the lovely manor, but as we sipped, almost unimaginably, the wine struck both of us as being vaguely carbonated. We looked aghast at each other and took another taste. And there it was again. Not like drinking a glass of soda water, of course, but not like savoring a nice glass of red wine, either.

What to do? If I were paying for the bottle, it should be returned, as it was clearly off. But if it were being offered to us at no cost as part of our host's generosity, then mightn't it be a bit much to declare it undrinkable and send it back?

Putting aside the reality that I had never returned a bottle before and felt horribly awkward about doing so now, to reject the bottle seemed a thoroughly ungrateful act. If we were going to refuse it, however, it had to be done immediately. We could hardly move on to the meal and then summon the waiter to inform him that we couldn't drink the wine. We were both in agony. I could hear the clock ticking.

The easiest option, of course, was to pretend everything was fine, drink the lousy wine, and focus on the food. That seemed to me both cowardly and morally wrong. If the wine were bad, I should be man enough to say so, no matter who was paying.

I decided to stand up for truth and asked the waiter if I could speak to the sommelier. There are few things snootier than a good English sommelier, and he immediately displayed his talents by reducing me to a stuttering bumpkin, apologetically attempting to explain what was wrong with the wine. Sniffing the cork imperiously, he stared at me as if it were entirely my fault. I made the case that the wine shouldn't be bubbly in any way. His retort, obviously taught him in sommelier school to silence contentious Americans, was magnificent: "A case of seasonal effervescence, isn't it, sir," suggesting that the mildly carbonated sensation was not a defect in the wine but merely a normal phase of its maturing before it reaches its desired end point of velvety smoothness. Believe that one, I thought, and I have a bridge....

I shrugged, smiled, and remained silent, unable to think of something convincing to say. Sommeliers are clearly under orders not to argue with guests, so having skewered me with this inspired absurdity, he scooted off, bottle in hand, and returned several minutes later with another. I assumed he had chosen a different vintage for us, one presumably not working through its sparkling development. But no, it was simply a second version of the same wine we had just turned back. He plunked it down on the table and disappeared. Why he thought it would be different from the first I can't imagine. It wasn't. More bubbles.

At this point I had no choice. Was the sommelier actually testing me? Had he made a bet with his colleagues that he could put one over

SEASONAL EFFERVESCENCE

on the ignorant American and get him to down the bad wine after all? Who knows? Whoever was paying for it, and however wretched I was feeling, now it absolutely had to go back.

I told our waiter that I needed to speak to the sommelier again. He returned to our table, and I explained that the carbonated experience was still the same, and I just couldn't drink it. I told him how embarrassed I was to have to say this, and he should know that I had never returned a bottle before. "Well, sir," he replied, "I would say you have done quite well, two bottles in one evening." (Scathing, if unfair, as it was really the same bottle twice.) But off he went, and this time he brought back a different vintage entirely lacking in the debilitating seasonal effervescence. I don't think I earned the admiration of the sommelier for my behavior, though I felt especially good about clinging to principle and maintaining my integrity when it turned out I was not paying for the wine.

Mr. P and Me

The thing about the prostate—or Mr. P, as I have come to think of him—is that he resents the lack of interest we owners generally show him. We monitor our blood pressure, we exercise our hearts, we check our eyes and our teeth and our hearing, we are sensitive to the temperamental behavior of our bowels. But the prostate? Come on. Few of us even know exactly where he is situated, or what humble task he performs. Sometimes we indicate our ignorance and indifference by pronouncing his name as if he had an additional *r* and were less an authentic gland than merely a recumbent condition. Left to ourselves, we pay him no mind. Under these circumstances, it is no wonder that he is eager to get us to appreciate his existence, to take him seriously. Given the distress he is capable of causing, it is prudent to try to understand things from his perspective.

If, as the real estate agents assure us, location is everything, it is hard to argue with Mr. P's unhappiness. Whether because of the implacable workings of evolution or the malignant impulses of an intelligent but mean-spirited designer, he has found himself relegated to a singularly unappetizing site: he clings grimly to the urethra as it comes from the bladder. No doubt there are worst places to be, but it is certainly hard to be enthusiastic about this one. At the very least, a low-rent neighborhood, not the sort to foster a positive self-image.

And then there is the issue of what he actually manages to accomplish. His sole function, not trivial, but not exciting either, is to provide much of the fluid that escorts the sperm out of the penis after it leaves its testicular home. A kind of car service that the male body dials up in the process of orgasm. Beyond this, Mr. P has nothing to do; the sad truth is that for most of the time, he is about as useful as the appendix. But whereas the appendix seems relatively well adjusted to its insignificance, Mr. P is most definitely not. He is angry at his tawdry surroundings, the amount of time he is forced to sit around, waiting for a call, and even his inconsequential stature, usually described as being roughly the size of a walnut.

Living with all these debilitating realities, he is consumed by one major obsession: to expand himself into the largest prostate he can be—say, the size of a grapefruit or, better yet, an elephant—thereby putting the demeaning walnut comparison behind him and earning our respect. And this is the problem. His insatiable desire for growth intrudes on systems and structures around him, causing all manner of disturbances, ranging from the merely inconvenient to the potentially fatal. If you can convince him that you admire him without his feeling the need to fill up all the extra space in your lower abdomen, then you are well ahead of the game.

But few manage this, impelling him to take action. There are, generally speaking, three kinds of steps he takes to remind us that he, too, matters. The first is what I call simple growth, of the sort that sends men scurrying to the bathroom in the middle of the night. Increasing his girth so as to restrict the urethra as it channels the flow of urine from the bladder, Mr. P figured out that the more difficult it is for the bladder to empty, the more often it will try to do so, leading to a state of sleep deprivation, which our CIA interrogators have long recognized as a valuable technique to obtain information from their detainees. When Mr. P's frustrations and desire for lebensraum finally lead you to your urologist (about this, more later), you will find that, most likely, the first question put to you is how often you must get up to pee at night. The answer to this will help the physician determine just how feisty Mr. P is.

The second question—also designed to evaluate his development—will invariably concern your urine stream. Here the keen urologist expects to hear that it is weak, erratic, scattered; he will look skeptically at you if you suggest, as I did, that despite the formidable size of Mr. P, my stream (the term of art in urology) was absolutely untrammeled, strong and true as Niagara Falls on a summer's day. He looked up from the history he was taking, and his eyes narrowed as he pronounced my stream the healthiest he had ever heard about from a man my age. I knew I was being both criticized and doubted—clearly it had no right to be that way—but I could only shrug and declare that I couldn't in all honesty describe it otherwise. Apparently my bladder's power matched Mr. P's growth, so as hard as he tried to squeeze shut, my bladder worked even harder to empty, resulting in the standoff that permitted me to sleep through the night.

In my case, stymied in his first efforts to call attention to himself, Mr. P then resorted to what I consider the second option: summoning a group of bacterial allies to render me miserable. If he wanted to make a statement, there could be no more powerful way than through a luxuriant, excruciatingly painful infection. Mr. P pulled this one on me about a dozen years ago. Having been impossibly healthy all my life, I had never seen the need for a doctor or a physical examination, so I neither possessed the former nor had been subjected to the latter. A throbbing pain in my side, an unappeasable need to urinate, and debilitating chills led me to believe that it was in fact time to see a physician, and a series of frantic phone calls to friends led me to my first urologist.

Sitting in his office, chatting amiably with the rather jolly doctor about my symptoms, I recognized Mr. P's devilish cleverness as a connoisseur of indignity. Not only was he causing me acute physical discomfort, but it became clear that he was also about to cause me to experience an act I had always hoped to avoid. As the doctor began to muse on my condition, I realized there was no escaping the dreaded DRE, or digital rectal examination, which had appalled me ever since friends of mine had first described it. That I had imagined that I could get through life without enduring it, of course, was a fantasy, but one I had nevertheless entertained. Staring at the urologist's immense fingers—they seemed as large as Coke bottles—as they played idly on his desk, I understood, courtesy of Mr. P, that my time had come.

I shortly found myself, minus my pants, draped over the examining table on my elbows, posterior in the air. Having reduced me to this condition of vulnerability, Mr. P was by no means through. With the probing mercifully brief and more unpleasant than actually painful, I thought I was over the worst. Mr. P, however, knew better. Standing up, with my pants still around my ankles, I was suddenly horrified to see my doctor, uninvited and unannounced, seize my racial organ (the euphemism preferred by Lord Baden-Powell, founder of the Boy Scouts) in one hand and begin rubbing it briskly back and forth on a glass slide he was holding in the other, as if trying to erase some intractable handwriting. Faced with a scene I found totally inconceivable, I fled to outer space, leaving my body behind. Looking down from above, I couldn't imagine what he was holding on to—was it a pencil? an asparagus? a cigar?—or what connection it had to me. I remained safely outside my body until the outrage stopped. I returned when the doctor instructed me, in a line I have never forgotten, to "clean yourself up, pull up your trousers, and we'll sit down and talk like gentlemen."

As I readied myself for the polite conversation, my urologist disappeared with the slide; several minutes later, he came back with what he announced as good news: I had a serious prostate infection. In response to my quizzical expression, he remarked that it was good news because otherwise he would have had to conclude, given Mr. P's bloated, spongy state, that I had cancer. I agreed that it was good news indeed—never had an infection seemed more welcome. A three-month course of antibiotics subdued Mr. P, and I once again ceased to think about him. This, it turned out, was a serious mistake.

Faced with my blithe dismissal, Mr. P clearly felt driven to exercise his last option, even at the cost of his own demise. He made his move some dozen years ago, when the blood test for my annual physical examination revealed an elevated level of prostate-specific antigen (PSA), a reading that pointed to the possibility of prostate cancer. My primary care physician, a superbly laid-back type who had little faith in the PSA test because of its history of false positives, thought that the spike in my numbers meant it would be appropriate for me to see a urologist. With the retirement of the doctor who had earlier spoken to me like a gentleman, this required a new recommendation, which in due course led to a tentative diagnosis, pending a biopsy, that Mr. P had in fact grown himself a malignancy.

But until the biopsy, we couldn't know for sure. Preparing myself for this event the night before brought with it its own special pleasure, namely the self-administering (more or less) of my first ever enema. I know that there are people—perhaps many people or even most people—for whom this would not be a problem, but I can only say that I am not one of them. Despite the cozy encouragement on the enema box about how the soft rubber tip makes for easy insertion, my body resisted with the same ferocity normally found in unsuccessful organ transplants. Twisting and turning as per the instructions to find the most "comfortable" position generated only degrees of unacceptable suffering. Try as I might, I could not manage to inflict this on myself, most of the saline solution dribbling uselessly onto the bed. I finally gave up, determining that it was the urologist's problem, not mine, and went to sleep.

The next day I arrived at his office, where I was greeted by his friendly medical assistant, who asked me how I was feeling. I responded that I wanted to run screaming out of the hospital. She assured me that this was perfectly normal, that most patients felt that way, and that all would be fine. I wasn't convinced, but decided that aggressively cross-examining her as to what basis she had for issuing such absurdities was not the way to go, so I simply nodded in agreement. She then sought to assuage my anxieties by explaining what exactly would take place during the biopsy procedure. She displayed a bizarre-looking instrument, about the size of a thumb, that would apparently take care of everything: at once an ultrasound probe, to image Mr. P on a screen; a supplier of anesthetic; and a gatherer of prostate cells through tiny needles, to be delivered to a pathologist.

If this was supposed to calm me, it didn't, but in any case I soon was stretched out on the examining table in the approved position: on my side, knees to chest, awaiting the arrival of yet another foreign object into my rectum. Perhaps as a means of avoiding the rather serious reality that this was the process that which would determine whether or not I had cancer, I found myself worrying that I might be chastised for having too much stool in my colon as a result of my enema failure. Nothing, however, was said about this, for which I was understandably grateful. As the probing and extracting begin, I attempted to relieve my extreme tension by making what I thought was a very funny comment: "I suppose this is not the first time you have done one of these," I said. No one laughed, and I decided it was best to remain silent and concentrate all my energies on relaxing. Silence proved much easier than relaxing, but in twenty minutes or so I regained sole possession of my rectum and now had only to wait for three or four days to get the pathologist's verdict about Mr. P's condition.

The urologist's certainty that in fact I had prostate cancer made the pathologist's report no surprise. Mr. P had played his trump card, and I was now officially one of the 250,000 American men annually diagnosed with this disease, which each year kills roughly 40,000. So I could be forgiven (at least I decided to forgive myself) my first, rather self-indulgent response to the news: "Am I going to die from this?" Moving beyond the melodramatic, however, with its accompanying "can it really be"s and "why me"s (when I could think of so many more deserving candidates), I realized I had to address this new reality and decide what to do about it.

Among the many unpleasant and potentially fatal illnesses that can afflict you, prostate cancer is particularly vexing in that no clear consensus exists regarding how best to treat it. Disparate therapies, with their committed practitioners, all compete for patients' business. There are the freezers (cryosurgeons who freeze the prostate to destroy the cancer cells); the seeders, who insert radioactive pellets into the prostate in a process known as brachytherapy; the beamers, who direct external beam radiation at the cancerous prostate; and the surgeons, who offer three different approaches to the removal of the prostate. Not to speak of the watch and waiters, who do just that as they monitor the progress of the disease.

Choice in life is generally regarded as a good thing, but for the prostate patient it is a source of confusion and even despair. How can one decide, since each treatment has its advocates and skeptics, its glowing successes and its statistical probability of complications, its risks of depressing side effects? Every prostate patient I have known—myself included—begins with the confidence that intensive research will resolve all questions and lead the way to a rational determination as to the absolute best method. The internet initially beckons us with its vast resources, and soon we are immersed in data concerning clinical trials, mortality rates, Partin tables, incidences of incontinence, Gleason scores, percentages of recurrence, European treatments, and addresses of innumerable prostate support groups. The more we explore, the deeper we become mired in information overload. Having sought illumination, we end as bewildered as ever.

The normal next step (or perhaps even the first, depending on your enthusiasm for internet investigations) is to call everybody you know—as well as those you don't know, once you hear about them—who had prostate treatment and find out what they did. The obvious problem with this approach, needless to say, is that they all did different things: I spoke to those who were watchfully waiting, who had been beamed or seeded or subjected to two different surgical methods. All seemed more or less satisfied with what they had done or were doing, so that their testimony was no help at all. And even if they hadn't been, it still would have been of no help (I came to realize), as their individual experiences bore no necessary connection to my own. Saturated with knowledge (one of the associated pathologies in having prostate cancer is the need to feel that you have done more exhaustive research about it than anyone else), I had absolutely no idea how to proceed.

Without understanding it at the time, I had reached that creative state of exhaustion in which I was actually ready to make a decision. The catalytic moment occurred when my physician son, who had been on the receiving end of my confusion in Cleveland, called to say that he had seen on the internet that a surgeon who had been recommended to me was giving a talk at a prostate support group on the East Side. He suggested I check him out. The thought of being reduced to one diseased prostate in a room of other diseased prostates did not appeal to me, and I angrily rejected the idea. Reflecting on this response, I was appalled by its stupidity. My delicate sense of individuality notwithstanding, there was no point in denying that for all practical purposes during this period I was in fact a cancerous prostate, struggling to figure out how not to be one, so I might as well hear what the surgeon had to say.

About a dozen men drifted into the small lecture hall to listen to the talk. I found myself gazing intently at each of them, trying to fathom if there was some mysterious prostatic bond I could feel uniting us. Stare as I might, however, they remained just a group of old men (I decided that they all looked considerably older than me, but that might have been simply my vanity), sharing nothing other than a disease. No revelation of spiritual affinity with my fellow sufferers was to be forthcoming.

Into this gathering of the ancient and infirm someone suddenly appeared who was decidedly neither: David Samadi, the surgeon we had come to hear. Young (not yet forty), handsome, with an elegant head of prematurely gray hair, and nattily dressed in a blue pin-striped suit and yellow tie, he radiated a confident, cocky energy noticeably at odds with the aura of genteel resignation I'd perceived in the room. Before he began his presentation, he suggested, as there were so few of us, that we all describe our current status with the disease. "I've been diagnosed and am watchful waiting," the first began. "I've been diagnosed and am watchful waiting," the second repeated. Ditto the third. My turn was next. I began to feel it was vaguely indecent of me to want to do something about my condition, since no one else seemed bothered by his, but I thought I would let Samadi know I was different. "I've been diagnosed, I was told to see you, and I am watching you very carefully," I said. He smiled. A good sign, I thought. After the rest had defined themselves, with several more watchful waiters, Samadi began his PowerPoint presentation.

None of my internet research or extensive conversations with old and new patients had ever touched upon the surgical technique he began to describe to us. Samadi is one of the leading practitioners of robotic prostatectomy, a method in which the surgeon removes the prostate through the use of a robot whose name, da Vinci, speaks to its mechanical genius. After making five small incisions in the patient's abdomen, Samadi inserts two minute cameras and two tiny surgical "arms," which he maneuvers by fitting his hands into the mitten-like holes of da Vinci's two stirrups, to cut what has to be cut, suture what has to be sutured, and remove the prostate with the least collateral damage to the surrounding nerves. The cameras provide magnification and a three-dimensional view of the operating field, enabling Samadi, concentrating on a screen on the robot, to work with exquisite precision. While the surgeon's individual skills, Samadi insisted, are still paramount for success, the unobscured view and firmness of manual control guaranteed by the robot are enormous assets in navigating in a rather congested and fragile space.

Samadi, at the time the director of robotic surgery at Columbia University's College of Physicians and Surgeons, followed his introductory remarks by comparing features of the three surgical techniques of prostatectomy: the traditional, or "open," surgery, in which the surgeon's hands enter the body to remove the prostate; laparoscopy, which permits the surgeon to operate outside the body through the use of fiber optic imaging and tiny instruments inserted into the patient, which are manipulated manually; and robotic laparoscopy, the option employed by Samadi.

I was astonished by the differences, particularly between the open and the robotic methods. Whereas there is considerable bleeding in open surgery, often requiring the patient to supply several pints of blood in the weeks before the operation, in case they are needed, robotic surgery minimizes blood loss. Four or five days of hospital recovery is normal for the open procedure, as opposed to one day for robotic. Two weeks of catheter insertion versus one (and in this sensitive area, believe me, every day counts) was another key point, as was a postsurgical complication rate of fifteen percent for open, which falls to five percent for the da Vinci, in the hands of an accomplished surgeon. The message was unequivocal: if you are thinking about surgery as a treatment for prostate cancer, robotic is the most reasonable—one is tempted to say the only—choice.

The facts were impressive in themselves, but equally impressive was Samadi's evident passion for his robotic procedure. Whatever the complicated mix of motives that drives people on in their professions, it was obvious to me that Samadi derived enormous satisfaction from having perfected a surgical technique that could rid patients of their prostate cancer. It was also obvious that he knew what he was doing, having completed approximately seven hundred of these operations. In addition to its ability to cure, he clearly loved working with an instrument as precise and efficient as the da Vinci. Narrating a videotape of one of his prostatectomies in which the robotic arms were about to perform a complicated task as they detached the prostate from its moorings, Samadi could not contain his enthusiasm: "Now this is the fun part," he exuberantly blurted out.

I left the hall that evening feeling I had at last found my way. Samadi and da Vinci both seemed right to me, a decision that, I realized, was as much visceral as intellectual. But since I'd already gorged myself on statistics and comparative analyses, trusting my emotions at this point struck me as sensible rather than irresponsible. Before I committed myself into da Vinci's mechanical hands, however, I thought I owed it to myself to speak to a "seeder" to learn about the virtues of brachytherapy. I made an appointment with a radiation oncologist who had previously treated a good friend, and saw him a week later.

Not surprisingly, he believed as staunchly in his method as Samadi did in his. Certainly he could make a strong case: the capacity to attack the cancer without the trauma of surgery, with results allegedly every bit as good as those obtained with surgery; no hospital stay or real recuperative period; no bleeding; and no incontinence (at least initially). And if it was good enough for Rudy Giuliani (I thought), who was I to prefer another treatment?

Against these real positives, there were also substantial negatives. As I've already indicated, my Mr. P had put on considerable weight over the years, and Dr. Seeder speculated on the desirability of shrinking him a bit with hormone therapy before inserting the seeds. When I expressed my lack of interest in growing breasts, he explained that a bit of X-ray treatment could handle that. He also pointed out that after the brachytherapy, it might be prudent to clean up the area with a touch more radiation.

None of this appealed to me; nor did the notion that incontinence, presumably absent at first, might possibly develop after a year or so. But perhaps my biggest reservations concerned the options available to me if, following the treatment, the cancer should return, as it does in a not insignificant number of cases. With the scarring induced by the radiation, dealing with the recurrence becomes a complicated medical problem for which, at that point, surgery is no longer the answer. So for the long haul (the haul I was hoping to travel), getting rid of Mr. P entirely seemed preferable to leaving him hanging around, zapped with the radioactive seeds. Besides, the lists of pros and cons notwithstanding, I realized that despite my efforts to keep an open mind, I had already opted for Samadi and his trusty robot.

The next step was to speak to Samadi, which I had not yet done, beyond throwing a few questions at him during his lecture. When Judith and I went to visit him in his neat office on Sixtieth Street (physicians always welcome mates when it comes to prostatic consultations), we both felt comforted by his marvelous confidence in himself and his technique. Not to speak of the experience he had gained from the approximately seven hundred operations he had performed. In an effort to convince myself that I was making the right choice, I feebly asked him why I should believe that surgery was a better therapy than the seeding. It was a meatball, right over the heart of the plate, and he responded by banging it out of the park. He wanted to cure me of the cancer, he stressed, and if I could explain to him why removing it was not the safest and surest way of doing that, then he would consider other solutions. It was, of course, what I wanted to hear, so I declined the invitation to argue.

But there was another issue that troubled me—as it does, I suspect, every man contemplating prostate surgery. Prior to 1982, removal of the prostate guaranteed impotence, as it was thought that the two bundles of nerves controlling erectile functioning had to be sacrificed with the prostate. But in 1981, Patrick Walsh, a young (forty-three-year-old) surgeon from Johns Hopkins, discovered that the nerves believed to run through the prostate were actually attached to the outside of it, allowing for the development of a technique to spare the nerves while taking out the prostate. After a year of study, Walsh was ready to try, and in 1982 he performed the first successful prostatectomy that left the nerves intact.

Walsh's method of nerve preservation, of course, rapidly became the norm for all prostate surgery. That it was now a possibility didn't mean, however, that it was always feasible—or manageable. If the tumor had spread outside the prostate capsule, for example, it might be necessary to excise the nerves as well. And in any case, the process of separating the nerves from the prostate required the utmost delicacy. Despite the best salvage intentions, a surgeon could inadvertently damage them permanently.

Naturally, Samadi appreciated my anxiety. He emphasized that his first obligation was to cure, and if the cancer had spread, he would have to take surgical steps to get rid of it. He also made it clear that if it was not necessary to remove one or both bundles, he would use all of his skill to save them. There was no other answer to give me, but I thought that with seven hundred procedures to his credit, he was in a position to deliver. I told him it mattered a lot. Already feeling that I had demonstrated sufficient incompetence in my life, and knowing that the operation would inevitably be followed by some incontinence, I was not eager to add a touch of impotence to the mix. He assured me that he understood what I was telling him.

As we left the office, I asked my wife what she thought. She was not about to be trapped by this, and asked me what I thought. I confessed that while it seemed weird to be enthusiastic about the prospect of surgery, which was not likely to be a pleasant experience, giving Mr. P over to Samadi felt like the way to go. I liked his straightforward, frank manner and, even more, his surgical background. Having begun his career by practicing open and laparoscopic methods, he had learned the art of the da Vinci in France, training with Dr. Claude-Clément Abbou, whom he considered the best laparoscopic surgeon in the world. Versed in all three techniques, he would, I was certain, be up to any of the challenges Mr. P might throw at him.

As my wife agreed with my assessment, there suddenly remained nothing left to do but actually make an appointment for the surgery. Samadi said that although he was booked up through December (it was now the beginning of October), there might be an opening sooner. I pretended to be pleased by this, but secretly I was counting on a few months of delay to prepare myself. I assumed, in any case, that sooner would mean sometime in late November. So when the phone rang on Tuesday, the tenth of October, to say that my surgery was scheduled for the coming Monday, I was irrationally angry. How could I possibly be operated on in six days? (As if anything more were required of me than to go into the operating room, lie down, get anesthetized, and let the wily da Vinci pluck Mr. P from my innards. But that, of course, was not the point. The point was, I was not ready, and I was furious with Samadi for accommodating me so promptly.) Thoughts of refusing the appointment occurred to me, but fortunately I resisted them. If I had to give up the luxury of marinating in self-pity and anxiety for three or four weeks, so be it. Mr. P and I would simply part company earlier than I had expected.

On Monday at one o'clock, wearing my funny hospital socks and crowned with the funny hairnet hat that adorns surgery patients, I was escorted to the very serious operating room where the da Vinci team awaited me. Two and one-half hours later I woke up in the recovery room, having gained five small incisions in my abdomen in the process of losing one overweight, malignant prostate. There was nothing surprising in this, as I had fully expected, pending some surgical mishap, to wake up without a prostate. What concerned me was less what Samadi had taken out than what he'd left in. Would my precious nerve bundles, in short, to which I had become so attached, still be both there and functioning? It was my faith that Samadi could manage this, after all, and that assessment had played a major role in my selecting him. Until I found out, I would be reluctant to celebrate the fact that perhaps I had been cured of cancer.

Several hours later, still groggy from the anesthetic, I was aware that Samadi had come to see me in my room. Croaking out the critical question, I received the surgical benediction I had been hoping for. "The nerves are fine," he pronounced, giving me the thumbs-up sign. I breathed out a Percocet-aided sigh of relief: there might in fact be normal life after the loss of Mr. P.

But not immediately. Certain consequences followed from the Samadi-led robotic assault on Mr. P and his stronghold. The first of these required the use of the catheter—another bodily violation that had always inhabited for me the realm of the entirely unimaginable, though I knew, of course, that this was a necessary part of the healing process. The reality was brought forcefully home the day after the surgery, as I was preparing myself for departure from the hospital. Before I was permitted to leave, I had to be instructed in the art of affixing to my thigh the small bag into which the catheter would drain as I perambulated about during the day. (Distinct from the large bag that would lie by the side of the bed as I attempted to sleep at night.) The skill was easy to master; the emotional impact that I would be living this tubular existence for a week (half the time, I reminded myself, of open-surgery patients) was not. Seeing a catheter protrude where no catheter had ever protruded before made me long for the days of Mr. P, when I could stand proudly before a urinal and choose consciously to relieve myself. While I tried to take comfort in the certainty that such times would come again—soon—I found it difficult to believe. Knowing that I was getting off lightly—one week instead of two—and that, in any case, it was hardly the worst thing that could happen to a person only added to my distress. I was thoroughly miserable. Had Dante known about this, I wondered, what group of sinners would he have imposed it on: bed wetters? fornicators? masturbators? exposers of self to little girls? I could conceive of no crime so heinous as to merit such a punishment.

Finally Monday, the day of my emancipation, arrived. I was to be liberated by an assistant of Samadi's named Helen, whom I immediately—and unfairly, as she was quite gentle and sympathetic—designated as Helen the yanker. Strapping on my portable bag for what I hoped would be the last time, I anticipated that there might be some humiliation in store for me, but I no longer cared. If CNN wanted to cover my yanking with commentary by Christiane Amanpour, that was fine with me. I just needed to be untethered.

Accompanied by my wife, who had been a staunch supporter throughout and was not about to miss this, I entered an examining room, where Helen instructed me to remove my pants and get up on the table. I confess I found being splayed out half naked before the approving eyes of my wife while another woman fiddled with my penis to be bizarrely unsettling, well outside the realm of any fantasy I had ever concocted. Under the stress, my mighty scimitar, the veritable battering ram of my masculinity, which had brought me such pleasure over the years, sought to flee the scene entirely. If it had not been tied to catheter and bag, I fear it might have been lost forever. Helen, who clearly had, as it were, seen it all and understood the anxiety attendant upon having the catheter withdrawn, kept making funny jokes about the screams of pain she'd elicited from even the strongest of men. I realized these lines were designed to put me at ease, but they exceeded my capacity to laugh. She commented that there seemed to be something wrong with my sense of humor. I didn't mean to disappoint her, but the fact was that along with other things, it, too, had gone.

She then explained that before she removed the catheter, she wanted to assess my urinary ability (if I failed, she sternly warned, I would have to be re-catheterized), and rather than have me drink many glasses of water and then wait, she could fill me up and test me right there. That seemed reasonable, so the next thing I knew, as I lay on my back, water was being poured into me via the catheter. Helen could somehow tell when the gauge read full, and as she continued to chat with me, she mentioned in passing that I was no longer catheterized. I had to admit—which I promptly did—that I hadn't felt a thing. Free at last. But now the moment of truth: Would I be able to urinate on my own?

Beckoning me off the table, Helen handed me a plastic urinal and told me to start peeing. Locating my tiny spout, which was doing its best to hide in my pubic underbrush, I aimed carefully and released. The miracle of urine started, and Helen was mightily pleased. But urinary health (or what portion of it one could hope for at this time) involved not just the capacity to begin but also the ability to stop. Helen gave me the order, and I squeezed as hard as I could to end the flow. It worked. Helen was full of encouragement and praise; my wife seemed quietly proud of her husband's fine achievement. "Release and stop again," Helen instructed. Again I performed brilliantly. "OK, now empty out." The examination was over: I had passed.

Exhibiting my urinary prowess before the careful scrutiny of two smiling females reduced me to a level of infantility I hadn't achieved since I was a howling newborn. If clearly I was not about to die for the sins of all mankind, I did at least feel that in my utter humiliation I was somehow atoning for all the ill-treatment men had perpetrated upon women since the beginning of time. Had the masculine world of exploiters, vilifiers, and degraders of women only understood the expiation I had just undergone on their behalf, I would have been, I am convinced, instantly canonized. As it was, in a small room on the eleventh floor of the Herbert Irving Pavilion, only three people witnessed this solemn ritual, two of whom had no idea of its true meaning.

With my capacity to urinate having now been officially certified, I was free to go home. Leaving the hospital un-catheterized was a blessing, but it instantly transported me to the ranks of the incontinent, an unavoidable change of status in the recovery process. For along with the necessary surgical trauma to the bladder involved in removing Mr. P, losing the backup support of his steely grip on the urethra makes it initially impossible to control the bladder as one formerly could. The resulting incontinence comes in all degrees of severity. At the worst (statistically a small group, roughly two to five percent of patients), the affliction involves a complete inability to manage, resulting in a debilitating, unstoppable urine flow, and at the best, the condition might be classified roughly as leakage. For a harrowing tale of the former, Michael Korda's *Man to Man* describes in grim detail his experiences of being literally awash in urine following his 1994 open surgery with the legendary Dr. Walsh. Although my condition, from the very beginning, fell into the latter category—I was spared adult Pampers, condom catheters, and the like—I found little comfort in that.

However marginal or temporary one's affiliation, membership in the fraternity of the incontinent brings with it no perquisites or privileges. Instead, there are only dues, which you pay twenty-four hours a day: depression; revulsion at your own body, which has chosen to betray you; obsession over whether you might be staining through your absorbent pad; an inability to focus on anything other than the proximity of the next toilet. In place of browsing in bookstores, you find yourself browsing in the incontinent section of drugstore chains, examining the latest variety of liner designed for your special needs. The simplest physical acts become treacherous: getting up from a seated position is dangerous; laughing or coughing courts disaster. Incipient dehydration can even be a risk, as you imagine (mistakenly) that reducing the intake of liquids will hasten your return to dryness. A corrosive anxiety about leaking affects not only what you drink (or don't—no caffeine, as it is a diuretic) but even your wardrobe. Light-colored pants, however elegant, are out. Trousers can't be dark enough.

In an effort to conceal, you actually become an open book to those who know you. When I reported to my insightful son in passing that I had recently purchased three pairs of jeans, he exhibited the diagnostic shrewdness that will serve him well in his medical career by inquiring what color they were. "Black," I said. "Hmm," he replied. "I wonder why."

With one alleged exception, there is little that can be done to encourage the bladder to behave obediently. That exception involves exercising the pelvic-floor muscles through a series of muscular contractions known as Kegels, named after their innovator, Dr. Kegel. I attach "alleged" to them because I have no way of knowing whether or not they work. Once I was told that they might, however, I became a virtual Kegel addict, performing my version of them obsessively throughout the day, lamenting only that I couldn't continue them while asleep.

Theorists of Kegeling abound, differing with one another as to both technique and preferred frequency, and I admit that I am entirely uncertain that I do them correctly. The basic idea is to tighten and release the muscles you use in stopping urination as a means of rebuilding the strength of the sphincter. In order to make sure you are contracting the appropriate ones, the internet, which is full of useful prostate information, suggests you slip a finger into your anus to determine if it is sufficiently clenched, a maneuver that I actually decided not to employ. Some experts argue that there are two sets of muscles that must be worked together, but this seems far too complicated for me. My primitive version is simply to squeeze and let go, and to do this whenever I can for as long as I can. Whether this counts as proper Kegeling or not, or even contributes to expediting bladder control, it at least has given me the confidence that should the occasion arise, and with my adrenaline pumping, I could, if I had to, bench-press three hundred pounds with my anus.

Whatever you do or don't, the bladder tends to dawdle along at its own rate, and it is almost certainly the case that patience is more important in the process of recuperation than even the most artful Kegeling. Four months after my procedure, my personal rainy season seems finally to be ending. As I lurch toward that divine state of aridity that I previously took for granted (but no more), I cannot help but think how Mr. P must have smiled to himself, even as Samadi's pincers closed in on him, knowing the difficulties he was going to cause me in the wake of his removal. It is part of his vengeful genius that, having endured my indifference during his lifetime, he made sure I would think of him every day after he had gone. And so I have. In rich postmodern irony, he has never been more present to me than since his absence.

As for my precious nerve bundles and their miraculous powers, it is too early to expect anything of them. The return of normal functioning can take as long as twelve to eighteen months, but I have no reason to doubt that the nerves are there, gradually readying themselves to serve my needs. Like the bladder, of course, they have their own schedule, one that couldn't possibly match mine. Even as

I grumble over the slowness of my rehabilitation, however, I can still hear David Samadi's response to some of my concerns at our first postsurgical meeting: "Last week you had cancer; today you don't." A point, I tell myself, worth remembering.

Hospital Madness

The diagnosis—postperfusion syndrome—is innocuous enough; the experience of it is not. Wikipedia, from which we laymen get most of our medical information, points out that it is also known as "pumphead," and describes it as "a constellation of neurocognitive impairments attributed to cardiopulmonary bypass (CPD) during cardiac surgery. . . . Studies have shown a high incidence of neurocognitive deficit soon after surgery, but the deficits are often transient with no permanent neurological impairment." What is missing from this accurate if bland description of the condition, which can follow bypass surgery, with its comforting assurance that the so-called deficits will eventually disappear without a trace, is the unimaginable suffering that patients caught in the web of dislocation and hallucination can feel before clarity returns. We are talking here not so much of neurological impairments as of unmitigated animal terror, a terror that is impossible to express but that requires exquisite understanding on the part of hospital caregivers about what the patient is going through. Realizing medically that the patient is in the throes of a known syndrome does nothing to alleviate the hellish torture that can be consuming the bypass survivor.

HOSPITAL MADNESS

I write, obviously, from personal experience, and I write both to inform those preparing for the procedure about a downside they should at least be aware of, and to make a plea for those caring for them to appreciate their potential pain. When I went into the hospital for an aortic valve replacement, it was determined that I would also require a triple bypass. My splendid cardiologist made it clear that he had spoken to me about the risks, but I confess I had not really digested his warnings. So essentially I had no idea about the possibility of impairment or disorientation, temporary or otherwise.

I emerged from the seven-hour operation with tubes in my throat, chest, neck, arms, and just about everywhere else. As I came into consciousness I apparently asked my wife if I were asleep or awake—a half-hearted attempt, I think in retrospect, to be funny, but probably also an indication of my tenuous grip on reality. The few days in the cardiac intensive care unit went by in a fog of sedation, and I have no particular memory of how I perceived myself and the world around me.

It was only when I was sent to a "step-down" room—a small single room one step down from the intense scrutiny of the CICU—that things became clear: the four nurses who were watching me were also plotting to murder me. I felt panicky and helpless—not a good combination—desperate to survive and horrified that I had allowed myself to get into this condition in the first place. I felt viscerally that I was too young to die, frantic about my vulnerability. When people are trying to kill you, of course, the only reasonable response is to try to escape, which in my case required me to get out of bed and flee. The problem was that I was too weak to get up from the bed, and whenever I struggled to do so, there was a gentle push on my shoulder from one of the nurses watching me (and, not unimportantly, planning to do me in), enough to undermine my efforts entirely, accompanied by the admonition to relax.

Relaxing, needless to say, was precisely what was impossible, since people were conspiring to kill me, and the advice only exacerbated my panic. Unable to extract myself unaided from the bed (presumably the site of my impending death, though I had no idea how it would be managed or, certainly, why), I conjured up a fiendishly clever strategy. There were some signs dealing with hospital matters on the wall facing the bed. Pretending they were paintings, I asked one of my guard-nurse-assassins if he would help me stand so I could look more closely at their beauty and intricate brushwork. I reasoned that once I was on my feet, I could suddenly bolt for the door and run to freedom. The unfeeling voice replied that there were no paintings and I should just continue to do what I could not do: relax. The firm shoulder pat guaranteed that I could not extricate myself from the bed. I asked the nurse if he was in fact planning to kill me; there was no answer.

I cannot be precise about the duration of this particular fantasy; I can only attest to the unspeakable anxiety it caused me. I had been released from the CICU on Thursday, so it must have started that evening. Sometime earlier—I am not sure when—I'd pulled out the arterial line from my wrist, and was told later that I had to be physically restrained during that first evening in the step-down room. Strange behavior, of course, to the outside world, but not if you are convinced your life is about to end. I was frantic to continue living. In the jumble of reality and fantasy that is my memory of this time, I distinctly recall putting my feet on one side of the bed, to facilitate getting up (which, of course, I could never accomplish), only to have the nurse push my feet back, after which I would place my feet on the other side, in an effort to elude him. Back and forth we would go, until I realized I couldn't win. It is possible that I imagined all of this, but it was real enough at the moment.

HOSPITAL MADNESS

The effort to remain alive was made more complicated by the fact that the nurses who were plotting against me seemed to have invaded my private living space. I was amazed and distressed that they had found their way into my apartment, and I demanded to know how they had gotten there. The argument that I was in the hospital and not home carried no weight with me, as I knew better. I then fashioned what I thought was a perfectly reasonable way to satisfy me as to where I was: Escort me to the door of the room, I asked, and permit me to look out. If I saw a hall, then I would know it could not be my apartment, and I could accept the reality that I was in the hospital. But with tubes coming out of my chest draining fluids into large canisters, no one was interested in my offer. I would have to take it on faith and the assurance of the nursing staff that I was in the hospital. I stayed unconvinced, though there was nothing I could do about it.

I also failed to convince anybody that I should be permitted to move my bowels in the solitude of a closed bathroom. This, no doubt, seems a minor matter, but it was not for me. I have always been quite private about my bodily functions, and the thought of defecating in public—or, at the very least, in front of a cadre of nurses—was literally impossible for me to deal with. Negotiations were futile. I could be permitted to use the bathroom as long as I kept the door open. Or a commode could be brought into my room. Neither option was satisfactory, and I continued to insist on my right to privacy.

At this point, everybody seemed against me, no one willing to support my claim. I was totally alone and became furious with all those who tried to reason with me about the dangers of moving about or being left alone. Foremost among my adversaries were my beloved cardiologist son, who had taken a week off from his busy practice in Cleveland to be with me, and my loyal and wonderful wife of forty-four years. Arguing with my son, I pointed out that he was not "my fucking doctor" and expressing his opinion was irrelevant. He properly had no say in my case. As for my wife, who remained adamant that I could not be left alone, I informed her that I no longer wanted to be married to her. She retorted, I distinctly recall, that we would talk about it later. (In the event, I didn't in fact need to use the toilet until I had taken several walks around the hospital halls, accompanied by my wife, thereby indicating my fitness to take care of myself. I was then cleared to go to the bathroom alone.)

My anger at my wife slid into what I know now to be a fantasy (but certainly didn't know then) that, in league with the murderous nurses, she had constructed a room with a glass-paneled wall between me and the bathroom, preventing me from getting to it. When I pointed out that she had no right to make modifications to our apartment—I still believed that I was back there, not in the hospital—she simply shrugged, declaring that she was helpless in the matter. Her refusal to intervene in my behalf only contributed to my need to end the marriage.

And so it went from the time I left the CICU on Thursday to sometime on Saturday, when the cloud of irrationality and anxiety in which I was living finally began to clear, and I realized that I was a patient in a hospital, that I was not on the verge of being murdered, that the nurses were on my side, despite my verbal abuse of them, and that I was not headed to a divorce proceeding. The period was exhausting, the gradual physical recovery from the seven-hour surgical assault on my body far less demanding than the emotional torment it generated. That my behavior could be categorized as a perfectly "normal" episode following bypass surgery did not begin to speak to the suffering I was experiencing. I realize, of course, that my set of fantasies was unique to me and by no means a generalizable pathology.

HOSPITAL MADNESS

Most people, emerging from surgery, no doubt. don't think they are about to be murdered. But whatever the distinct forms of anguish that can plague postperfusion survivors, I would like to attest to their crippling reality. Physicians and nurses who encounter them should appreciate that the need to sedate and restrain, while inarguable, does not address the overwhelming terror in which the patient may well be immersed. I don't know what can be done about it, as there is clearly no way to penetrate anybody's inner reality to grasp what is going on, other than to realize that the pat on the shoulder and the exhortation to relax are not going to make things better.

A Bad Scout?

The New York Review of Books, June 28, 1990, issue

IN RESPONSE TO:

"Boys Will Be Boys" from the March 15, 1990, issue

To the Editors:

In his review of Tim Jeal's biography of Baden-Powell [*NYR*, March 15], Ian Buruma refers to my book *The Character Factory* as one of the best known of the "leftist" or "progressive" efforts to debunk the Chief Scout's mythology, and praises the ease with which Mr. Jeal handles my "conventional, progressive" views of Baden-Powell. While I appreciate that "progressive" is intended to be intellectually disreputable in this context, I confess to being surprised by the labels. I had thought the point was to understand, even if the understanding involved some unpleasant truths.

Take, for instance, the question of Baden-Powell's racism, which I raise in my book. Following Mr. Jeal's lead, Mr. Buruma dismisses the subject with the knowledgeable claim that "B-P was no more racist than most Englishmen of his time, indeed in many ways less." (How Mr. Buruma knows the degree to which most Englishmen of the time

A BAD SCOUT?

were racist remains a mystery, but no matter.) The issue, of course, is not whether Baden-Powell was more or less racist than anyone else, but whether his racist thinking tells us something important about the originator of a significant social movement whose professed ideals transcended race.

So it won't do to be cozy with it, as Mr. Buruma is, or worse, as with Mr. Jeal, to pretend it doesn't exist. Jeal's ability to explain away the offensiveness of Baden-Powell's frustration at native sloth in forming a levy (*The Downfall of Prempeh*, 1896)—"The stupid inertness of the puzzled negro is duller than that of an ox; a dog would grasp your meaning in one-half the time. Men and brothers! They may be brothers, but they are certainly not men"—is a hermeneutic triumph which does not disturb Mr. Buruma in the least. It turns out to have been simply a mistake, indeed the "common European mistake," Jeal writes, "of supposing that Africans whose way of life did not require the punctuality of factory workers were too stupid to run their affairs in an organized fashion" (162). That this mistake is a splendidly incisive definition of racism does not seem to have occurred to Jeal, or to Mr. Buruma.

In addition to misunderstanding the benign and homey nature of B-P's racial beliefs, I was apparently also led astray by my progressive blinders over the issue of scout militarism. For Mr. Buruma, "Jeal's argument that B-P's Boy Scout Movement didn't have military aims may be quite correct, in fact is correct; what the Chief Scout aimed at was to revive the warrior spirit in peacetime, rather like the old samurai and his Bushido." It is hard to know where Mr. Buruma draws the line between reviving the warrior spirit and what is conventionally understood to be militarism. As I tried to demonstrate in my book, B-P was himself incapable of making that distinction. A lifetime army officer, he not surprisingly saw the military virtues of obedience and loyalty as comprising the basis of all human excellence.

Scouting explicitly developed out of the trauma of the Boer war and the anxieties it unleashed concerning the deterioration of Britain's manhood. One of the ways Baden-Powell sold the scouts to the nation was by stressing the critical role they could play in preparing the rising generation for the next war. As he cautions at the start of Scouting for Boys, "Every boy ought to learn how to shoot and obey orders, else he is no more good when war breaks out than an old woman."

To accept the militarism of scouting's origins and early ideals is not to undercut the value of scouting or to suggest that it didn't develop in different ways over the next eighty years. But why must we pretend that its origins were not what they were?

Finally, as a debunked debunker, I would like to point out a major scholarly blunder on my debunker's part which Mr. Buruma overlooks. Mr. Jeal is adamant—and Mr. Buruma seems to agree—that Baden-Powell was oblivious to class concerns and that the scouts were not in any way intended as an instrument of social control to help secure the loyalty of the poor who stood essentially outside the social system. In this regard, it is interesting to see that when Jeal reproduces the original scout law of 1908, he prints the second stipulation as follows: "A scout is loyal to the King, and to his officers, and to his parents, his country, and his employers" (392). In fact, "parents" were not included until the 1912 version. The omission was not accidental. Baden-Powell viewed the parents of the under classes as part of the problem, rather than respectable figures of authority to whom he could trust his scouts. It was only when scouting clearly emerged as a middle- and lower-middle-class movement that B-P felt it was appropriate to require scouts to promise loyalty to their parents. Such was the jovial "boy-man's" innocence of class matters.

Death and Friendship

As my mother grew older, her elderly friends, naturally enough, began to die. She would talk to me about their loss and what it meant to her. Much to my everlasting shame, I remained largely indifferent to her pain. After all, she was still alive, and that was what counted. The disappearance of friends, sad to be sure, could not be construed a major disaster. So I listened to her complaints, but without much empathy.

Now that I am at the age she was when she died, and my once-rich trove of friends has been replaced by a vast array of gravestones and urns, I am astonished by my insensitivity to her unhappiness. How could I have been so callous? How could I not have realized that the loss of trusted friends is in fact a major disaster, leaving us exposed to the elements as we hadn't been before? This past year, for example, witnessed the end of three relationships, one of an older friend, one my age, and one substantially younger, a former student. One hundred and fifty years of phone calls, dinners, laughter, shared memories, emotional support—all wiped out, forever. The death of friends may not be the worst thing we have to deal with in our lives, but it's not trivial, either. I can't believe I didn't appreciate my mother's suffering.

SCRAPS, ORTS, AND FRAGMENTS

My first personal encounter with death involved a family member: Uncle Willie, my father's older brother. Allegedly somewhat of a roué, according to my highly judgmental parents, he married Aunt Evelyn because her family ran a successful lingerie business, then treated her abominably; he had numerous women, didn't go to college, and drove a flashy Cadillac—all signs of serious moral failure for the uptight Rosenthals. But I liked him. He was fun, he played with me, took me to football and baseball games, shared my passion for sports. If he didn't meet my parents' behavioral standards, he certainly met mine. When he died in the hospital, of an aneurysm that probably should have been caught and repaired but wasn't, I comforted myself by thinking that after all he was an old man (probably somewhere in his sixties) and that family deaths were to be expected.

Aunts and uncles followed in due course, but none was particularly close to me and none affected the quality of my life. They were no longer at holiday gatherings, but I can't say they were exactly missed. The first awful death I experienced, one that tore a gaping hole in the fabric of my existence, was that of a younger friend, a former Columbia student. Jody had taken several classes with me, and we had become extremely close. He was a man of brilliance and wit whose ironic sense of things mirrored my own. Rarely did a week go by in which we didn't talk to each other at least several times. He called me "my dean," although I wasn't, having been appointed associate dean after he graduated from the college. But I think he liked the idea of elevating me into his own private authority figure. It was also, of course, a joke.

Judy and I had gone to Mexico for a few days at the end of February 2005. We stayed at a simple hotel on the beach that didn't have a phone in the room, lolling about in the sun, keeping cool in the bay and hotel pool, drinking mojitos and margaritas. A perfect, relaxing vacation. On the third day, there came an early-morning knock on the door. I opened it, to be handed a note: "There is a phone call from your son Noah in the office. Please get it immediately."

There was no way that a seven a.m. call from Noah could be a casual event, so I ran. I heard the words he was saying when I got to the phone, but they made no sense: "Dad, I have terrible news—Jody Pope is dead."

"How? Why? What happened?" I blurted out, unable to understand what I was being told. Jody, I learned, had apparently returned from a picnic on a Saturday afternoon, didn't feel well, and thought he would sleep in a guest room so as not to disturb his wife. When she woke up on Sunday morning to look in on him, his eyes were rolled up in his head and he had lost consciousness. Rushed to the hospital, he died later that morning.

Healthy young men—Jody was only in his early fifties—do not just drop dead of natural causes in a day, my cardiologist son Noah emphasized, and although two autopsies were unable to determine the reason, he was convinced that Jody had to have been poisoned. As melodramatic as this sounds, there was no satisfying medical explanation to otherwise account for his sudden extinction. No aneurysm, no stroke, no heart attack, no exotic infections, no strange viruses.

If Jody's health was fine, his law practice had taken him in several different directions in which his death would have been welcomed. One was a multimillion-dollar suit he had brought against tobacco lawyers he claimed had defrauded the plaintiffs they were representing. The other was a Russian mafioso he was defending against criminal charges but whose case he had lost, an outcome that Russian mafiosi tend not to appreciate. So was he poisoned and, if so, by whom? No one knows, and autopsies, as Noah insists, make clear what didn't happen, not necessarily what did. All we know is that my beloved

Jody disappeared from my life with no explanation and no warning. A precious friend, a major loss. He did at least leave me with a final message on my home phone, which I found when I flew back to New York for his memorial service. "My dean," he said, "I have an idea for a new novel. It's called *The Last Bar Mitzvah*." It never would have been written, of course, but I have always regretted not having had a chance to talk to him about it.

With the exception of an occasional suicide (and Jody's sudden, unexplained end), the ineluctable pattern of diagnosis, prognosis, and condolence notes tends to conclude most relationships. Few surprises, no miracles. The amount of time you are permitted to invest in one friendship or another remains the critical variable. Of the three friends I lost this year, Richard had been struggling against multiple myeloma for a long time. We both knew what he was going through, discussed the nature of the experimental drugs he was taking, incorporated his vulnerability into our conversations and interactions. We were never oblivious to the strict limitations of our time together. We had no way of knowing when he would die, just that it would be too soon, and that he would be the first of us to go, was clear.

Harvey, by contrast, was both older than either Richard or me and had never been ill for as long as I knew him. He sometimes joked that he had no intention of dying. We would meet for lunch regularly on the Upper West Side. The last time we met, he said he wasn't particularly hungry, as he had just had a late breakfast, so I ate a sandwich and he had an espresso. He was going to Greece the next week and then to London to gamble, an activity he loved. We agreed to see each other when he returned. He never went to Greece, though I didn't know that. Instead he died of metastatic lung cancer, which had spread throughout his body. He knew he was dying when we got together. It wasn't that he wasn't hungry, it was that he couldn't eat. While that knowledge would surely have been difficult to deal with, I wish I had been told. I hate the fact that I said good bye not realizing I would never see him again.

The third irreplaceable loss this past year involved another former Columbia student with whom I had established a nourishing friendship. We discovered each other while I was in the administration and he an editor at the *Spectator*. He earned my everlasting admiration by coining in the pages of the paper the delicious description of the British dean and his trusty associate dean as "the British-Yiddish combination."

Dan went on to become a hugely successful lawyer, and when making money no longer seemed worthwhile, he left law to start a program to guarantee computer access to New York inner-city kids. His brilliance, humanity, generosity, and commitment to others made him a very special friend. So when I learned that he had contracted Creutzfeldt-Jakob disease, a fatal brain disorder of rapid deterioration and no treatment, I was distraught. Given the brevity of the lifespan following diagnosis, if I wanted to communicate with him, I was warned, it would have to be soon, very soon, as it was not clear how long he would be alive or able to understand anything. To lose a dear younger friend whom I had privately put down to speak at my funeral was traumatic enough. To face a pressing deadline in an effort to conjure a final message, neither saccharine nor maudlin, to explain to Dan how much we admired and loved him, seemed almost impossible. I had written my share of sympathy notes to surviving spouses and children of friends who had died. I had never written to a friend who was actually in the process of dying—and in as cruel a way as one could imagine—with time running out.

Somehow I managed it. While my words obviously wouldn't change the dreadful fact of his impending loss, it was critical to me that I got through to him. One of those small achievements that mean everything. I was immensely gratified that I had succeeded. What I didn't expect, of course, was any sort of response. Knowing Dan, I shouldn't have been surprised. The same day I wrote my email, I received an answer: "Wish I knew how to send on this device the tears of joy and sadness wafting through my failing brain, dear precious Michael and Judy. Processing very hard, but devotion as strong as can be. Bless you and thank you. Love, Dan."

Although it must be statistically true that death accounts for the majority of the ends of relationships among the elderly, I don't mean to suggest that there aren't a myriad other reasons. Long associations can bring with them fissures and strains that take time to surface, and that a friendship can't necessarily survive. In my case, two sad examples speak to the disparate ways in which relationships can deteriorate.

The first was with a colleague in the English department, arguably my closest friend there. He was bright, funny, delightfully irreverent—all qualities dear to my heart. We played tennis and squash together, enjoyed bad movies, engaged in endless family dinners. Yet even as our friendship flourished, I began to detect, over the years, an oddly utilitarian feature to it. Maurice loved departmental gossip—I did as well—and our frequent phone calls would invariably begin with his sharing what he had learned about maneuverings and affairs in the department, then demanding, "And what do you have for me?" Which, I understood, referred to nothing in my life but to what information I could provide him about our colleagues.

Every now and then, as a test, I would slip something personal into my report, about which he proved entirely uninterested. He wanted to know about others and the life of the university, not about my existence. Hardly my conception of how friends treated each other. But while my evolving understanding of the role I played with Maurice significantly tempered my enthusiasm for our relationship,

DEATH AND FRIENDSHIP

I still liked him and did my best to supply him with whatever compelling gossip I could uncover. Over time, as Maurice grew increasingly important in our profession and increasingly self-important, I became accustomed to the varieties of minor indignities that arose in our interactions, but none were so severe as to make me question the point of the friendship.

About fifteen years ago, the English department began actively recruiting Hermione Lee, a distinguished British biographer teaching at Oxford who was spending the semester in New York. Maurice, who had gotten to know her, decided he could push the process along by inviting her to dinner. He confided to me that he thought a successful evening might well succeed in tempting her to come to Columbia. The critical issue, then: Who should the other guests be, those who could be counted upon to bring the requisite gravitas and fascination to pry her loose from Oxford?

A month or so before Lee Day, the phone calls began in earnest. The provost certainly, perhaps the vice president, maybe the department chairman, certainly Edward Said, our most eminent faculty member, probably Jean Strouse, director of the Cullman Center at the Public Library, where Lee had a fellowship. How about some bright junior faculty to show her the talent coming up? We have room around the table for only ten people, Maurice pointed out, so we have to get it right. Professors from other departments or just English? The questions were endless as Maurice explored with me all the possibilities, day after day. Throughout the conversations, one name that was never mentioned was mine. I understood. I wasn't on Maurice's A-list of stars and, despite our close friendship, was judged to be insufficiently important to impress Lee. (I could have argued with this ranking, since, like Lee, I had written a book on Virginia Woolf. But I certainly didn't expect to be included among the august few who might bring Lee to Columbia.)

Several days before the event, disaster struck. Said was ill, the provost couldn't make it, Strouse had to be out of town. What was Maurice to do? Examining his shrinking options, he decided the B-list was acceptable. "Would you come?" he asked rather haltingly over the phone.

"No," I replied.

"You're not angry with me, are you?" (More than anything else, Maurice hated having people mad at him.)

"No, I am not. I know where you are coming from, but I will not be there."

The dinner party went ahead, though without the level of distinction Maurice sought. Who knows whether a provost or two would have made a difference, but Lee is still at Oxford. Maurice never spoke to me about the evening.

When I told Maurice I wasn't angry with him, I was telling the truth. That I was found worthy to consult about the guest list but not qualified to attend did not endear Maurice to me. If it didn't make me angry, it certainly announced, to me at least, that time was running out on this friendship.

Several years later, time entirely expired. The decisive event on this occasion was a party to which I was actually invited, a book party celebrating Maurice's latest publication. As a veteran book party attendee, I am familiar with the protocol. You go, chat up the other guests, nibble on a few hors d'oeuvres, and congratulate but make sure not to impose yourself on the author, who is busy working the room. I don't need guidance on how to behave. But Maurice wanted to make sure I knew my place. "You understand," he pointed out over the phone when telling me of the party, "that I won't be able to speak to you."

So I could attend, but he would take no notice of me. I wouldn't have gone, but I was curious to see the select people to whom he would be devoting his attention. And there they were: Robert Caro, the preeminent biographer; Eric Foner, the distinguished American historian; and a smattering of other literary and academic notables, who apparently maintained a higher rating on the importance scale than I did. I suspected they hadn't received a similar cautionary phone invitation. Indeed, I might well have been the only one there to require special instructions. Warning me what to expect (or, perhaps more accurately, what not to expect) marked a fitting end to our friendship.

My second non-disease termination of a long-term relationship (fifty years or so) was precipitated by a self-published memoir written by my friend Richard, who sent me a copy. It focused on his travails as an English graduate student at Columbia in the sixties and a young single man on the Upper West Side in search of love. I enjoyed reencountering the girlfriends I'd known then and the funny, pathetic episodes we'd all experienced in our early twenties. What I didn't enjoy was the characterization of me as a calculating careerist who, "unlike me," according to Richard, never liked teaching and therefore turned to administration to get ahead, whose "signal achievement" in seventeen years as associate dean was to change an outmoded rule regarding the granting of the grade of incomplete, and who chose to write a biography of the president of Columbia because he knew the university press would publish it (never mind that it was published by Farrar, Straus & Giroux).

Richard explained that I had "hated doing it" but that it had "paid off" for me. In fact, when I wrote the book, I had long since returned to being a professor, and I received no benefits other than the satisfaction of finishing a project on which I had worked for a dozen years.

I was startled by the animus, not to speak of the factual errors, particularly as regards the publisher of my Butler book. I immediately wrote him and let him know I was appalled by the depiction of me, which was so filled with untruths. How could he have said such things? And why?

He answered by stressing that he hadn't meant to offend me, and had he known, he said, "how extreme your reaction was going to be, I think I'd have done things very differently."

I pointed out that I wasn't offended, I was angry, and the two were not the same. I was angry because he had said things about me that were not true, and that he presumably must have known were not true. Otherwise, what did he mean by declaring he would have done things differently had he anticipated my reaction?

He finally said he agreed with my anger and apologized, though he never addressed his reasons for writing about me as he did. The more I thought about it, however, the less his apology seemed serious. His portrait of me was not haphazard or a function of sloppy prose or lack of attention to detail. It constituted a deliberate attempt to present me as a reprehensible figure always on the make. Why would I want to be friends with someone who viewed me this way? I decided I didn't.

The loss of friends, either by death or conscious choice, represents an inevitable reality for which we are generally ill-prepared. When I think back to the large number of friends Judy and I maintained early in our lives, to the weekends when we would actually throw dinner parties on both Friday and Saturday evenings, I see that it never occurred to me that it would ever be different. I recognized that parents would, of course, eventually disappear, but friends? Surely with an endless, renewable supply, friends would always be there. If not requiring two dinner parties over a weekend to handle the crush, certainly one.

Now there is no crush to be handled, and no dinner parties, either. As the circle of human contact closes around us, I am reminded of my mother's sadness and of her letting me know, though I don't think deliberately, what was in store for me.